Solutions for Creating the Learning Spaces Students Deserve

Embracing a
Culture of Joy

Dean Shareski

Solution Tree | Press

Copyright © 2017 by Solution Tree Press

All rights reserved, including the right of reproduction of this book in whole or in part in any form.

555 North Morton Street
Bloomington, IN 47404
800.733.6786 (toll free) / 812.336.7700
FAX: 812.336.7790

email: info@SolutionTree.com
SolutionTree.com

Printed in the United States of America

20 19 18 17 16   1 2 3 4 5

Library of Congress Control Number: 2016949141

ISBN: 978-1-943874-12-5 (paperback)

Solution Tree
Jeffrey C. Jones, CEO
Edmund M. Ackerman, President

Solution Tree Press
President: Douglas M. Rife
Editorial Director: Tonya Maddox Cupp
Managing Production Editor: Caroline Weiss
Senior Editor: Amy Rubenstein
Copy Chief: Sarah Payne-Mills
Proofreader: Kendra Slayton
Text and Cover Designer: Abigail Bowen
Editorial Assistants: Jessi Finn and Kendra Slayton

This book is dedicated to my wife, Paula, who chooses every day to make her classroom and our home places of joy.

Acknowledgments

I never considered writing a book. I'm a blogger, and I have always recognized a blog as a place where people with a thought or idea could say whatever they wanted, however they wanted. Books are reserved for people who really know what they're talking about. (And who don't end sentences with prepositions.) Yet it's nice when others think you worthy of this medium. Thanks to all the people who have read my blog over the years, whether you intended to or not. I consider it a mild endorsement.

Specifically, I'd like to thank those who have given me opportunities to grow professionally. My colleagues at Prairie South School Division gave me a chance to explore the affordances of technology both in my classroom and as a consultant. Richard Schwier mentored me during my graduate studies and continues to do so. Alec Couros invited me to teach, and together we've coined the phrase *lazy professors*, who take full advantage of networks and the gift economy. Lance Rougeux and my team of coworkers at Discovery Education are the most gracious, kind, and supportive people I know. To those whom I have connected with online and whom I learn and laugh with every day in various spaces—you know who are.

My family gets most of the credit. Paula, Meredith, Sam, Shea, Martha, Matt, Curtis, Alanna, Larry, and Rosa: thank you for your love and support and constant reminders of joy. I'd also like to especially thank my mom, who passed away twenty years ago and gave a talk called *A Celebration of Joy* to her women's group a year before she died of cancer. Finally, I want to thank my dad who has been my example of what it means to live a life of joy.

Solution Tree Press would like to thank the following reviewers:

Steve Kane
Principal
James Bowie High School
Austin, Texas

Paige Sanders
Principal
Woodland Park Elementary School
Sheridan, Wyoming

Yolanda Rios
Assistant Principal
San Jacinto Intermediate School
Pasadena, Texas

Melissa Torrence
Science Teacher
South Garland High School
Garland, Texas

Table of Contents

About the Author

 **Dean Shareski** is the community manager for Discovery Education Canada. He taught grades 1–8 for fourteen years and spent nine years as a digital learning consultant for Prairie South School Division in Moose Jaw, Saskatchewan. In addition, he has taught and designed courses both at the University of Regina in Saskatchewan and at Wilkes University in Pennsylvania.

Dean's blog, *Ideas and Thoughts*, consistently ranks among the top educational blogs. He also blogs for *Tech and Learning* and *The Huffington Post*. In 2010, he won the International Society for Technology in Education (ISTE) Award for Outstanding Leader of the Year.

Dean has had the opportunity to speak to a variety of education audiences within the United States and Canada as well as outside North America. He believes humor and humility go a long way in supporting and advocating transformational practices in teaching and learning. More important, his efforts to promote joyful learning and working environments remain his greatest passion.

He holds a master's degree in educational technology from the University of Saskatchewan. Dean has been married to Paula for over thirty years, and together they celebrate their four children and their families. When not teaching and sharing, you might find Dean on a golf course.

To learn more about Dean's work, visit his blog, *Ideas and Thoughts* (http://ideasandthoughts.org), or follow @shareski on Twitter.

To book Dean Shareski for professional development, contact pd@SolutionTree.com.

Foreword

By William M. Ferriter

Can I ask you a tough question? How many students in your classrooms are truly satisfied with the learning spaces you have created for them? If your students reflect the national average, the answer is bound to be discouraging. Fewer than four in ten high schoolers report being engaged in their classes, and students often list boredom as the primary reason for dropping out of school (Busteed, 2013). Over 70 percent of students who don't graduate report having lost interest by ninth grade and, worse yet, the majority of dropouts are convinced that motivation is all that prevented them from earning a diploma (Azzam, 2007).

These numbers are troubling for anyone passionate about schools. They indicate systemic failure on the part of practitioners to inspire learners and warn us of the immediate need to transform education—a warning that school leadership expert and series contributor Scott McLeod (2014) issues:

> If we truly care about preparing kids for life and work success—
> *we need schools to be different.* If economic success increasingly
> means moving away from routine cognitive work, schools need to
> also move in that direction. If our analog, ink-on-paper information
> landscapes outside of school have been superseded by environ-
> ments that are digital and online and hyperconnected and mobile,
> our information landscapes inside of school also should reflect
> those shifts. If our students' extracurricular learning opportunities
> often are richer and deeper than what they experience in their
> formal educational settings, it is time for us to catch up.

Scott is right, isn't he? Our schools really do need to catch up if they are going to remain relevant in a world where learning is more important than schooling— and catching up can only start when we are willing to rethink everything. We need to push aside the current norms defining education—that teachers are to govern, direct, and evaluate student work; that mastering content detailed in predetermined curricula is the best indicator of student success; that assessment and remediation are more important than feedback and reflection; that the primary reason for investing in tools and technologies is to improve on existing practices. It's time to implement notions that better reflect the complexity of the world in which we live.

That is the origin of this series. It is my attempt to give a handful of the most progressive educators that I know a forum for detailing what they believe it will take to *make schools different*. Each book encourages readers to question their core beliefs about what teaching and learning look like in action. More important, each title provides readers with practical steps and strategies for reimagining their day-to-day practices. Here's your challenge: no matter how unconventional these ideas, steps, and strategies may seem at first, and no matter how uncomfortable they make you feel, find a way to take action. There is no other way to create the learning spaces that your students deserve.

Introduction

In 2011, I was invited to participate in a unique experience called UnPlug'd. It was a gathering of forty educators from across Canada who were very connected and very "plugged in." With the purpose of exploring the big question of what really matters in education, we spent the better part of a weekend on a remote lake in northern Ontario completely disconnected from the outside world. Each of us came with our own story or idea. I had been immersed in technology and had witnessed first-hand the way it had changed many of my views about learning and the possibility of something different for schools. Yet, as I pondered what matters, I kept coming back to the simple notion of joy.

As a student, I didn't really like school but loved learning. I didn't hate school; it was merely a rite of passage to adulthood. The idea that school should be a pleasurable experience was nonexistent. That's not to say it never was fun—fun just wasn't a priority. In some cases, fun was seen as the antithesis to real learning. I never really challenged this belief as I began my teaching career in the late 1980s. Whenever I did experience moments of joy as a student and a teacher, the inevitable question emerged: Why isn't school like this all the time? Of course, as the routine of the day returned, I suppose I relegated joy to a *nice but unnecessary* component of school. I was wrong.

Sitting at that remote lake, I realized that learning and joy are inseparable. Real learning always includes joy. Sometimes joy needs to be sought out and experienced if learning is to take place. As I considered what I believed mattered most, I could not escape the word *joy*.

The group came together and cowrote an education manifesto, *UnPlug'd: What Matters Most in Education* (Siemens et al., 2011), on what we believed were the most important ideas for change.

During the writing of my brief chapter, I had the privilege of collaborating with and getting great feedback and questions from my writing partners. My colleagues probed deeper into my beliefs and asked me to consider why joy meant so much. I thought about my own habits and actions as a classroom teacher and realized that while I was by no means as diligent and intentional as I should have been, I often deviated from the grind of the day to make time for joy. Some of my proudest moments were seeing students smile, laugh, and become immersed in an activity. I realize now that those moments needed even more attention and care.

Since I began my career as an educator in 1989, many things have changed. In particular, schools are under much greater scrutiny by various stakeholders, including businesses and governments, who continue to see schools as essentially workforce-preparation factories. As economies continue to struggle and change, the debate about how schools can fix this problem rolls on. Without question, schools play a part, but they have always played a larger role in students' lives. The notion of *educating the whole child* is not new, and yet it often gets lost in our efforts to focus on what's easy to measure—grades, standardized tests, and other quantifiable data like attendance—as well as the mandate to ready young people for the workforce. Many teachers have pursued this profession because they've found learning to be pleasurable. Schools were not just a way to gain employment but also the complete community experience of learning, and learning with others was indeed joyful.

I'm interested in creating a place where we think about schools as a preparation for life, not just work. Certainly this is an arduous task and one that will not provide clean data that fit neatly into spreadsheet cells. Yet, I continue to believe this is our true mandate. In the end, I hope we equip students with a variety of skills and dispositions not only to earn a living but also to build a life worth living. When it comes to learning, the objective is to see learning as a joyous and wondrous journey that never ends. A lofty goal for sure, but one I believe is right.

About This Book

The idea of joy is a somewhat elusive concept, and even though it can come upon us quickly and organically, we can also create the conditions for joy to surface and ultimately become part of the culture.

As a blogger for over a decade, I've come to love writing in the blogosphere. For me, it's been a conversational space where I'm able to share half-baked ideas and thoughts and receive feedback from friends and strangers alike. I've often said that it's been my best professional development. So writing a book with real editors and publishers like a grown-up means I probably need to sound like I have more authority and expertise than I actually do. Some of what I share is personal and some is anecdotal. This book may not be filled with hard data, but if you want to be challenged and encouraged, I think you might find this book useful.

I invite you to see this book as a conversation. My goal here is to share more about the idea of joy—where we may have lost it and continue to lose it, and some practical ideas for getting it back. For many, this book might reawaken the very reasons you chose the profession. Others may realize that what they've been doing all along is really about joy but perhaps they haven't been able to articulate why they do what they do. Or maybe you're reading this because you are skeptical and see joy as a superfluous idea that waters down and is a cheap substitute for rigorous learning. Whatever your perspective, this book is meant to start a discussion. Here's what we'll discuss.

Chapter 1 examines the expectations and language of school and how certain terminology may negatively impact students' perceptions of learning. Chapter 2 defines joy and its effect on learning. Then, we'll explore a few elements that I think are key to embracing a culture of joy. It isn't a definitive list, but it makes a great starter kit for deeper conversations. Chapter 3 explores educators' *unfair advantages*—unique strengths they bring to schools. We'll embrace wonder in chapter 4, and in chapter 5, we'll discover the importance of play. Chapter 6 stresses the benefit of making school a community. Chapter 7 demonstrates the connection between gratitude and joy. Finally, the conclusion encourages readers to *just go for it* and cultivate joy whenever possible. At the end of each chapter, I've also provided Questions to Explore as a means to inspire a conversation about embracing a culture of joy.

I will say that I'm unwaveringly passionate about the idea of joy in the classroom, and I invite you to test my ideas and thoughts and decide what role they might play in your world. You are more than welcome to continue a conversation about this topic with me at any time. I reside in many spaces online and would love to connect with you in the same way I've connected with so many folks online through my blog and elsewhere. Being able to discuss ideas is much more important and interesting than expecting an expert to simply tell everyone what to do. I look forward to hearing where I may have helped you as well as where I may have gone wrong in my thinking.

Let's get going.

Chapter 1
The Expectations of School

We have to stop thinking of an education as something that is delivered to us and instead see it as something we create for ourselves.

—Stephen Downes

How would you describe the state of education today? Are schools better places for students than they were when you were a student? In some ways, they are. Great teachers are able to utilize a richer library of resources, and technology—when used effectively—creates unprecedented opportunities. In other ways, however, I wonder if we've lost something. Our obsession with analyzing test results and measuring learning has done its share of damage to students and teachers alike. But nostalgia is often a skewed lens to view the past through. Corporal punishment, a lack of resources, and an emphasis on lecture and memorization were not exactly ingredients for creating cultures of joy. However, in my opinion, teachers and schools faced fewer restrictions and less scrutiny from the public, making it easier to pursue joy. This lack of accountability certainly had its downsides, but today, increased emphases on standardized tests, public reporting of school results, and media coverage have teachers and schools walking on eggshells. The slightest stray from the curriculum can attract unwelcomed attention. Specifically, schools' overemphasis on standards and the general language of school can negatively impact culture and, therefore, learning.

An Overemphasis on Standards

Today, almost everything a teacher does needs to align to curriculum standards. As a beginning teacher, I know I wouldn't have been able to articulate it, but my decision to do fun things was based on the idea that the relationship with my students trumped the curriculum. Over the years, I've done many classroom activities with students because I thought they would be fun. I certainly didn't refer to my curriculum guide to see if they fit with any particular standard or outcome. It wasn't that they were opposing purposes but simply that relationships came first. As National Teacher of the Year Jeff Charbonneau (2014) shares, "Relationships then content. Both matter. So does the order." However, teaching the curriculum and finding joy are not necessarily competing ideas—teachers just need to find the right balance. Even simple ideas like using games to teach concepts like multiplication tables can provide smiles and excitement while still targeting required outcomes.

Several specific moments have shaped my belief and influenced my thinking about the importance of joy.

I taught grade 1 for the first seven years of my teaching career. In 2010, my family and I moved to a new house, and as I rummaged through old class pictures, I came across a photo of the very first class I taught. One student whom I immediately thought of was Christine. Christine rarely smiled. Twenty-five years later, that was the one thing I clearly remembered. I wonder if she smiles today. I'm not worried about her reading or whether her mathematics skills are up to par. I'm not even worried about her career. I wonder if she has any joy.

In 2011, I stumbled across a *lip dub*, a video that combines lip synching and audio dubbing, that college students created (Vaughn, 2009). Lip dubs were still pretty new then and remain an extremely creative digital genre of storytelling. As I watched, I thought, "I want to do this with students." My excitement over the lip dub was quickly challenged as I shared my plan with others. At the time, I worked with a small group of district-level consultants. When I showed them the video, many wondered where it fit into the curriculum. Some liked it but felt it would be better done as an extracurricular activity. A few dismissed it as a waste of time. These reactions reminded me that our beliefs about learning and school vary greatly.

A third moment happened as I walked into an elementary school and heard an out-of-tune piano being played and students singing. It was a sound I hadn't heard in a long while. This wasn't a music class but just a group of students and a teacher who believed singing together was good. I remember thinking, "We don't hear much singing in schools anymore." Billy Joel talks about the times he'd been to England and visiting pubs, and inevitably, he'd be asked to play something on the piano. He says that music "creates community, instantly" (WNYC, 2012).

One final moment came in late 2011. I was giving a keynote at Tech Forum Texas (Shareski, 2011b), and a small part of my talk referenced joy. Overall, I felt I had done very poorly. I hadn't given many talks at this point and struggled to create a cohesive message that I felt would be useful. I understood that joy was something powerful that resonated deep within people yet was largely ignored in education. Even as clumsily as I shared its importance, I hoped it was going to be a theme that would be shared often.

Later that day, a second-grade teacher found me and thanked me for my message. She had recently lost her son, who was killed in Iraq, and was understandably finding it difficult. She recognized that her grief was impacting her students and didn't think there was much joy in her classroom. She realized that needed to change.

These moments point to one idea: joy. Christine reminded me that I want students to love learning and love school. I'm not so naive to think that all students will love school all the time. But if we're going to use phrases like *lifelong learning*, school has to be an enjoyable experience. While I also know that Christine's lack of joy was likely due to many other factors, I spent five hours a day with her and was disappointed that I wasn't successful at bringing a smile to her face very often. The fact that we live in a time of unprecedented access to content means we see new things like lip dubs and can explore them and replicate them. It's not likely that we will see the words *lip dub* in any curriculum documents or standards. Yet the opportunity to play and make things with new media should certainly be seen as valuable. Doing things together, like creating videos or singing, has the underlying ability to build community and connectedness. Building community in schools and classrooms needs to move from a platitude to something intentional.

With the emphasis on standards and sticking to the curriculum, schools have become riddled with specific terminology about student achievement—perhaps the wrong words. This terminology almost always refers to test scores and grades and, more specifically, improving test scores and grades. However, improvement almost always begins with culture. *Culture* has become a buzzword in education and rightly so, but like with *lifelong learning*, school culture has to be an enjoyable experience. As Peter Drucker says, "Culture eats strategy for breakfast" (as cited in Rick, 2014). This idea suggests that people's beliefs and expectations about an organization are much more powerful than any stated plan or mission statement. I would suggest it also implies that behaviors and attitudes will do more to influence success than your stated plans. Creating a culture of joy, or anything for that matter, requires both intention and commitment. The great thing about culture is, as Tony Hsieh (2009) of Zappos says, "If you get the culture right, most of the other stuff . . . will happen naturally on its own."

So we might say that joy hasn't really gone away—when it comes to schools, it's never really been there. But that's debatable. That said, joy and learning have always gotten along. The good news is that there is a shift to move away from a focus on teaching to a focus on learning. However, I'm still not seeing an acknowledgment of and a focus on the beauty and joy of learning.

The General Language of School

Perhaps the biggest barrier is the language we use to talk about school. Joy can be a bit like exercise. We recognize its value, but many don't take time for it every day. According to Arja-Sisko Holappa, a counselor for the Finnish National Board of Education, there's an old Finnish saying that's fitting for education: "Those things you learn without joy you will forget easily" (as cited in Walker, 2015).

Language and words matter. Education is full of jargon that gets used to such a degree that we either dilute or modify its meaning, at which point we are unaware of its often deleterious impact. For years, students have been asking the age-old question, "Why do we have to learn this?" The typical reply is often, "You'll need it for the next grade." While this answer is true, it's another way in which we advance the bureaucracy of education and dismiss the notion that learning for the sake of learning is a joyful and beautiful experience. When we think about learning, it shouldn't bring fear or dread but joy and excitement.

In *The Book of Learning and Forgetting*, Frank Smith (1998) provides a clear argument that learning is something we all do naturally. The questions become, Are we learning what is important, acceptable, and useful? Are we exploring new things that challenge us and help us grow as learners and humans? This is where the role of school hopes to provide guidance. Curriculum is essentially an arbitrary guide of skills and knowledge. Others decide what's important and charge teachers with ensuring students learn it. While it's easy to argue whether everything in school is necessary, it's safe to say there is plenty that truly is important for students to know. Yet somehow, educators have filed much of their teaching under *it's our job* rather than *this is fascinating*. This culture permeates our schools, which affirms for students that school is boring. It has become something that is done to them rather than something they perceive as useful and interesting.

It's no wonder that students continue to see school as onerous when many of the words we use elicit images of drudgery. These words and phrases create unnecessary and harmful stereotypes that I'm not sure we always recognize. Many of these are impacting students, and just as many create a less-than-desired work environment for our teachers. Let's take a look at just a few.

Rigor

Of late, there is a big movement toward *rigor*. This interesting word deserves a closer look. If you look the word up in the *Merriam-Webster Online Dictionary*, you'll find the following definitions:

> 1a (1): harsh inflexibility in opinion, temper, or judgment: severity (2): the quality of being unyielding or inflexible: strictness (3): severity of life: austerity
>
> b: an act or instance of strictness, severity, or cruelty
>
> 2: a tremor caused by a chill
>
> 3: a condition that makes life difficult, challenging, or uncomfortable; *especially*: extremity of cold

4: strict precision : exactness <logical *rigor*>

5a *obsolete*: rigidity, stiffness

b: rigidness or torpor of organs or tissue that prevents response to stimuli

c: rigor mortis (Rigor, n.d.)

I struggle to find a definition that I would feel comfortable ascribing to learning. Yet the word has taken over in many districts as a point of pride. Many schools have built their mission statements around this term and use every opportunity to brag about the rigor in their schools. I can understand what people would like the word to mean, but I don't know why we would choose that word. Alfie Kohn (2004) writes about it in "Feel-Bad Education: The Cult of Rigor and the Loss of Joy." In it, he asks a question from educational researcher and theorist John I. Goodlad—"Why are our schools not places of joy?"—and goes on to discuss people's affection with rigor (Kohn, 2004). The belief seems to be that unless learning is hard, it's not worth doing. I don't know why we've associated hard with important, but this is clearly a dominant belief. After all, we might be embarrassed if people thought of school as easy. Instead, we make every effort to announce our schools as rigorous. Teachers often brag about how difficult their courses are as if that alone makes them valuable. Memorizing a phone book would be hard, and, dare I say, rigorous, but not nearly as meaningful as learning to play a game with others in gym class. Along those same lines, because classes like gym and art are often more enjoyable, they're seen as less valuable. Similarly, a class like trigonometry is a challenge for many and consequently viewed as more important in our hierarchy of subjects. I would argue the majority of the things I've learned in life have been very pleasurable and a natural consequence of being in a healthy learning environment exploring something I was interested in. Learning isn't best described as rigorous. Learning is when we desire to understand and create. Certainly learning can be challenging, but the goal of learning shouldn't be difficulty. We want students to be able to handle difficulties and struggles, but this becomes a much more palatable experience when the work is meaningful. The use of the word *rigor* sets a tone for schools. It's not a word that inspires learning but one that evokes a strict and narrow view of learning. Kohn (2004) also states, "I'm appearing to accept an odious premise—namely, that joy must be justified as a means to the end of better academic performance. Not so: It's an end in itself."

I'm not suggesting we don't embrace difficult, challenging work. I'm not even suggesting we don't look for it. But we don't need to lead with it. If the work we do with students is meaningful and important, I don't think we'll want to describe it or label it as *rigorous*. *Challenging, complex, meaningful,* and *purposeful* are all better ways to describe learning.

Accountability

Another term that has become part of the educational lexicon is *accountability*. Derived from business, *accountability* made its way into schools through the standardized testing movement (Hursh, 2001). Schools and teachers must now prove their worth in more direct and visible ways. Teacher evaluations enforcing accountability are often linked to test scores and even school-based funding. While it's difficult to argue that accountability isn't important, it's both a matter of process and product that we need to address. Accountability is almost always a top-down, hierarchical structure. Leaders and policymakers decide what measures and standards should be met and charge teachers in making them a reality. Whenever we hear the term, there's a subtle, and at times not-so-subtle, message that "you're not doing your job." There is tremendous value when a school shares accountability and develops collaboratively. Richard Elmore (2002) states:

> Accountability must be a reciprocal process. For every increment of performance I demand from you, I have an equal responsibility to provide you with the capacity to meet that expectation. Likewise, for every investment you make in my skill and knowledge, I have a reciprocal responsibility to demonstrate some new increment in performance. This is the principle of "reciprocity of accountability for capacity." It is the glue that, in the final analysis, will hold accountability systems together.

However, this is not the norm. A huge part of accountability in education revolves around measuring student success and, more specifically, achievement, as defined by test scores. The complexity of student growth and achievement has been diminished in favor of simplistic and easily aggregated data. An emphasis of product over process continues to pressure schools and teachers into doing only things that will improve test scores. The so-called *soft skills* of questioning, collaboration, problem solving, and creativity, among others, have been reduced to results and data that can fit inside a spreadsheet. Teachers have less time and less inclination to focus on a student's individual needs and growth; instead, they must place more energy and effort into raising test scores. What is being lost in our efforts to meet these demands?

In 2014, Ellen Best-Laimit, the interim principal of Harley Avenue Primary School in New Jersey, sent a letter to parents informing them that the annual kindergarten performance would be cancelled:

> Dear Kindergarten Parents and Guardians:
>
> We hope this letter serves to help you better understand how the *demands of the 21st century* are changing schools, and, more specifically, to clarify, misconceptions about the Kindergarten show. . . . Although the *movement toward more rigorous learning standards* has been in the national news for more than a decade, the changing face of education is beginning to feel unsettling for

some people. What and how we teach is changing to *meet the demands* of a changing world.

The reason for eliminating the Kindergarten show is simple. *We are responsible for preparing children for college and career.* (as cited in Strauss, 2014; emphasis added)

Obviously, this is a district that believes in accountability dictated by very narrow measures. However, the cost of accountability is great. When teachers feel they're not doing their job right, trust is the first thing that goes. How teachers feel matters. The concept of accountability should be scrapped or at the very least revisited to be reciprocal, where teachers and students have the opportunity to show the depth and breadth of their learning. Some of the most important skills students learn will never show up on a test, and yet these are skills that help students succeed in life. It's almost impossible for leaders to fathom an education system that does not embrace accountability. How will we ensure student success?

As many people look to Finland as a model of education success, it's interesting to note Finnish educators don't use the word *accountability* at all. In fact, Pasi Sahlberg, a former policy advisor for Finnish education, states, "Accountability is something that is left when responsibility has been subtracted" (as cited in Partanen, 2011). It's difficult to find joy in your work when someone else is mandating much of how you're assessed and what and how you're teaching. Of course, many would argue that's the way the world works. As an employee, you should be expected to meet the standards your employer sets. This is true for the most part, and educators would not argue with that statement. However, student success is a complex, nuanced experience that goes well beyond a single test. This complexity is best addressed in collaboration with those working directly with students: teachers. Continuing to use the word *accountability* as something done to teachers and students only leads to disengagement and even animosity toward those enforcing the rules. Through disengagement and animosity comes initiative fatigue. It's an acknowledgment that perhaps we've overloaded our goals and expectations. The idea is that teachers should carefully choose a few goals and be relentless in pursuing them. Therefore, unless a school's activity is aligned directly to achieving the goals, it shouldn't be considered. Purpose and focus are necessary, but a data-driven approach too easily ignores the fact that we're dealing with human beings, and developing ones at that. Changing accountability to responsibility or even an emphasis on reciprocal accountability would increase the likelihood of including broader and richer means of determining success. Doing joyful things might be the most important work we do. And when leadership in particular makes it clear that joy for joy's sake is important, then culture begins to change. Maybe we can be better, more humane, more just, and more joyful than the real world. What a great lesson and model for our students.

College and Career Ready

College and career ready is another mantra spreading throughout our schools. Although it's a seemingly positive and important mission, I see two major issues with this theme.

First, it tends to ignore that schools serve many purposes. Horace Mann's education model, which is the foundation of our current public system, was established to fill factories with workers (Rose, 2012). The unwritten agreement between schools and parents had been "You take care of the social and emotional aspects of your children, and we'll look after the academics." Over the years, this agreement has been tempered, and we've recognized that schools need to do more than simply teach content. Regardless of who's responsible for students' emotional development, we know that learning becomes more difficult when students suffer from emotional, social, and physical challenges. While the debate as to who should take responsibility for these needs remains unresolved, schools do have a greater purpose than simply enabling students to find work. The college-and-career-ready focus might be a step back as it indirectly diminishes important benefits of a public education. I like the idea of *future ready* as a way to update our teaching to do a better job of preparing students for the new world of work, but *college and career readiness* is too narrow.

The second issue I have with the term is the intensity and pressure it places on students and schools. As Best-Laimit states, "We are responsible for preparing children for college and career" (Strauss, 2014). Remember, she's speaking about five- and six-year-olds. Playing in the mud, painting, running, and singing have no place in this skewed version of the world. Without intending to, we're robbing students of their childhood. When someone tells five-year-olds that they need to be thinking about their future, or even tells this to their teachers, we create a culture where play and the joy of childhood are replaced with preparing for adulthood. The influence of business and society to compete in a global economy creates schools where students are forced to relinquish their childhood and get on with the serious business of life and making money. Indeed, part of the purpose of school is to prepare our students for college or careers, but it is every bit as important to prepare them for a life of learning. Sadly, it would seem we've accepted the fact that life must be a stressful existence, so why not begin it while we're young? Studies show this continues throughout high school with as many as half of students saying they experience a great deal of stress on a daily basis (Leonard et al., 2015). The major sources of their stress? Schoolwork, grades, and college admissions. Do we eliminate these? Maybe not, but do these need to be causing undue stress? When learning is joyful, stress does not dominate the culture. (Also, see Jain, 2015, for some positives of stress.)

The good news is that leaders are beginning to acknowledge this unhealthy obsession with grading and its harmful effects. David Aderhold (2016), superintendent of schools in West Windsor-Plainsboro Regional School District in New

Jersey, acknowledges the negative impact of grading and frightening levels of stress in a letter to his constituents:

> Perspective seems to be gone as we keep pushing the education system to the point where we—and, I mean the collective we (parents, teachers, and students)—have created a system where learning takes a back-seat to academic success. The grade has become the end point, not the learning. (p. 2)

Early education is a wonderful way to jump-start a life of learning, but many programs simply jump-start a life of schooling. We need to be careful that school remains a place that nurtures the whole child rather than one designed to prepare students for a life of testing.

Student Achievement

Student achievement is the last phrase I'll investigate that has become commonplace in schools. Many policymakers and the like have made it clear what schools should value. Michelle Rhee's controversial career included many firings and a singular focus on test results as the measure of success, which led her to become chancellor of Washington, DC, schools. She is often seen as the poster child of the new reform movement. The new reform movement's supporters look for easy fixes to the education system. Rhee believed toughness that centered around stringent, direct instruction would lead to increased test results. Her early years as an educator reflect her beliefs about school and learning:

> I wore my game face. No smiles, no joy; I was all thin lips and flinty glares. . . . My mistake the first year was trying to be warm and friendly with the students, thinking that my kids needed love and compassion. (as cited in Lemann, 2013)

Joy would not likely be a word to describe her tenure. In a *TIME* Magazine article, she states:

> The thing that kills me about education is that it's so touchy-feely. . . . Don't get me wrong. Creativity is good and whatever. But if the children don't know how to read, I don't care how creative you are. You're not doing your job. (as cited in Ripley, 2008)

"Creativity is good and whatever." I don't know about you, but when I read that, I'm thankful my own kids aren't in her schools. To her, test scores are the pinnacle of success, which is often masked by the phrase *student achievement*. Leaders and policymakers talk about the desire to improve student achievement, but when pressed, they almost always refer to some type of test score. Standardized tests continue to remain controversial, and even as districts try to downplay their role, student achievement is still the goal. When test results only represent student achievement, it's simply a bait and switch. When we focus on test results, we certainly impact culture. Students, teachers, and parents become driven to make decisions that serve to increase those scores at the expense of many valuable and important opportunities.

We tend to value what we measure. In the case of our schools, we value numbers and grades. We do little to recognize the other things that matter. We are inundated with bottom-line thinking, making creativity and a love of learning secondary to high test scores. In a world that needs innovators, creators, and problem solvers, we may be focusing on the wrong things. Yet we tend to celebrate students based on grades and award ceremonies that remain focused on numbers. We should focus on something better—a love of learning. What if we recognized students for loving learning? Perhaps we should give a joyous learning award, a persistent learner award, or perhaps a wonder seeker award? If indeed we say we value these traits, being intentional about honoring and celebrating them would certainly elevate and promote them in building our desired culture.

Let's be clear: it's not that these words and phrases are bad in and of themselves. But there is no question that words have meaning, and through our actions, these words impact our attitudes and beliefs about teaching and learning. Consider Bill Ferriter's (2015) tweet: "Would visitors to your school walk away convinced that learning is an inherently joyful act worthy of celebration?" Certainly, no one intends to create a joyless classroom environment, but the way we speak and think about learning greatly influences and establishes school culture.

Questions to Explore

- What words or phrases do you hear in your school or district that immediately evoke a strong emotion? Can you articulate why that is?
- How do we deal with existing concepts like accountability and student achievement to create more palatable experiences and richer meaning?

Chapter 2
The Definition of Joy

Joy is what happens to us when we allow ourselves to recognize how good things really are.

—Marianne Williamson

If we're going to talk about moving away from a focus on standards and toward one on embracing a culture of joy, it's important that we define *joy*. While there are a few definitions we might choose, I'm going to focus on these (Joy, n.d.):

> 1a: the emotion evoked by well-being, success, or good fortune or by the prospect of possessing what one desires
>
> b: the expression or exhibition of such emotion

Joy isn't about being happy all the time. It isn't a fleeting emotion that comes and goes depending on changing circumstances. It is about contentment and satisfaction and expressing those feelings. Sometimes that expression is visible, and sometimes it's not. But joy requires an awareness that things are right. While it's a deeply personal state, it's also something that, when given the opportunity, will spread. Creating a culture of joy applies to both the environment and the learning itself. As it relates to learning, it's the outward manifestation of success, achievement, and being. It's learning for the sake of learning, not because of a grade or compliance. These are the moments we naturally seek.

Identifying Joy

The good news is that our schools are still full of joyful moments. Perhaps we don't always acknowledge them as such, but they are there.

Consider the following.

- When the bell rings and students don't leave because they are in the midst of an engaging conversation

- When students are fully attentive as the teacher reads them a story

- When students cheer at the success of a third try at a science experiment

- When students smile because the class cheered them on in the gym

- When a student recognizes the beauty of nature

- When a teacher asks students about their soccer game

- When a teacher acknowledges a student as an expert

- When a student solves a difficult problem

- When a student comes in early to work on a project

All these things and countless others happen every single day. Most times they are forgotten as quickly as they occur. Sometimes they are deemed as unimportant. It's imperative that we create a culture where the possibility or the prospect of attaining success is evident. Instead of passing these moments off as incidental, we need to be intentional in capturing these moments and sharing them with each other. Rob Fisher, a principal in northern Manitoba, shares a twenty-second video of him working with an autistic student (Shareski, 2016). Like many principals, Fisher realizes that a student's well-being extends way beyond his or her grades and curricular activities. He actively seeks ways to create joyful moments. Fisher was teaching the student to play AC/DC's "Back in Black" on the guitar. Fisher worked the fret and chords, and the student strummed the rhythm. The look on the student's face in the video is pure joy: "the emotion evoked by well-being." The message from this moment is far greater than the moment itself. It signifies that this was worth sharing. It demonstrates to the student that this was important. It shows the school that while this was perhaps not part of any curriculum, it mattered.

Engaging learning environments are naturally joyful places. These are places where taking risks is encouraged and pursuing personal interests is expected. I realize that *engagement* is often used to describe ideal learning, but I would argue that joy has perhaps a higher purpose and one that is an outcome of engaging learning. Engagement can be a catalyst, but joyful learning is the real goal. Joyful learning is something even our youngest learners understand and experience. As mature learners, we may need to tease out this idea in our own lives and draw on our experiences to articulate and identify the joy that comes from new learning. While learning is certainly not a state of constant euphoria, school culture can be joyful. Those students who wake up each morning excited to go to school may indeed be going to a place where joy is the dominant culture. It's about safety, belonging, and hope. When we meet these basic needs, we can focus on new opportunities to learn.

Making Joy a Cultural Experience

In Daniel H. Pink's (2009) book *Drive* and Barry Schwartz's (2015) book *Why We Work*, both authors effectively argue that people's satisfaction with their work is based on purpose, autonomy, and mastery. Their research points to the power in making the shift to a more purposeful, autonomous work life and a cultural experience rather than an individual pursuit. While these ideas apply to adults and work, I see no reason why these wouldn't apply to students and schools as well.

If you simply see joy as somewhat superfluous or a way to water down learning, you're missing the fact that it's a requirement for learning. The cofounder of the NeuroLeadership Institute, David Rock (2008), says:

> Engagement is a state of being willing to do difficult things, to take risks, to think deeply about issues and develop new solutions. . . . Interest, happiness, joy, and desire are approach emotions. This state is one of increased dopamine levels, important for interest and learning. (p. 3)

As Judy Willis (2014) states, "Joy and enthusiasm are absolutely essential for learning to happen—literally, scientifically, as a matter of fact and research. Shouldn't it be our challenge and opportunity to design learning that embraces these ingredients?"

Most would be fine with using *joy* to describe learning for young students, but as they age, it becomes a more debatable, or at least a less-valued, notion. For many, it can be seen as almost demeaning to true academic pursuits as it seems to devalue learning. Yet, for others, it's a welcome return to the essence of what great educators do and have always done. It points to a more human endeavor that recognizes the link between emotion and intellect—again, a simple three-letter word that perfectly captures the reason many choose this profession in the first place. Education has complicated a very natural human experience; *joy* is a wonderful word that focuses on and so fully describes a state of being and a culture that few people in any circle would speak against. Consider using joy as a way to take back learning and make it the beautiful thing that it is.

Questions to Explore

- Think of a joyful moment. What led up to it? Have you shared that with anyone?
- What are the consistent, ongoing elements of your school or district that you see as joyful? How are you using these to amplify or enhance a culture of joy?

Chapter 3
The Unfair Advantage

Thank goodness I was never sent to school; it would have rubbed off some of the originality.

—Beatrix Potter

Alex Blumberg, journalist for *This American Life*, tells the story of his attempts to get funding for his new startup (as cited in Feloni, 2014). He met with an important venture capitalist to convince him to invest a significant amount of money in his new business. He prepared by developing his business plan and a presentation that clearly outlined the company's intent and projections. When the time came to deliver his pitch, Blumberg fumbled awkwardly through his attempt to describe the plan's details. The investor stopped him and told him he wasn't interested in the plan's details. Instead he asked a very unusual question: "What's your unfair advantage?" In other words, what qualities, experiences, and passions did Blumberg have that set him apart from the competition? This question wasn't something Blumberg was initially prepared to answer. He had all the data and financial details that would surely convince anyone he had a good idea. But the investor wasn't interested in that. He wanted to know what made Blumberg special.

Inhibiting Factors

As I listened to this story, I realized that educators could consider the same question: What's your unfair advantage? As I've been asking teachers and leaders alike that question, I often get very perplexed reactions. There are three reasons this question seems a bit out of place to educators, though I would argue it may be a powerful place to begin as we seek to create more joyful learning environments.

1. **Isolation:** Teaching is an isolating profession. While we've begun to recognize this and attempt to change it, for the most part, teachers

spend a large part of their time with students and have little or no interaction with other adults. They may be across the hall from colleagues, but once the bell rings, they are typically on their own. Conversations and opportunities to discuss and share practice are still rare, and while structures like professional learning communities are attempts to rectify this, teaching, overall, remains an isolated existence. This is why it's difficult for educators to see how they may have qualities, experiences, and passions that create unique and memorable learning experiences.

2. **Humility:** Even if they do see something about their practice that sets them apart, teachers are part of a culture of humility that prevents them from openly sharing these successes. To the detriment of authentic and meaningful sharing, educators have a fear of being seen as braggarts and avoid tooting their own horn. Certainly, the Internet and social media have empowered teachers to share, but there still exists a caution to appear in any way as a braggart.

3. **The science of teaching:** Teaching is both an art and a science. However, the emphasis has been and is increasingly about teaching as a science. From the extreme practices of scripted lesson plans to the subtler pressures of common assessments, districts and policymakers have attempted to create more homogenous environments to ensure consistency in all classrooms. However, this often removes the artistry and celebration of unique classrooms. We tend to focus on how to do things more alike and resist the notion that classrooms should be different.

The third point may be the biggest one. What if teachers thought of themselves as artists first? What if they considered what they bring to teaching that is special? What if they had an unfair advantage? If you think of a musician, you tend to focus on what he or she does differently from others. Yet to be a great musician, you also have to understand and have very good technique. You have to be well versed at the science of music. Good musicians watch and learn from others to improve their technique. And yet, what makes them special and what keeps them coming back is the artist in them. As fans, we love what makes them unique and special. We like different artists not because of their similarities but mostly because of their differences.

Leaders can play a role in helping teachers identify their unfair advantages. The concept *positive deviance* (see Positive Deviance Initiative, 2016; www.positivedeviance .org) examines what makes some people with access to the same resources more successful than others. Often, they have no idea what they do differently. These things happen in schools every day, particularly as they relate to the intangibles of teaching. The way teachers interact with students, the techniques they use to set up their rooms, or the skills they use to help students beyond their comfort zones are typical examples of great teaching practices that go beyond the lesson plan. If you ask them how or why they do these things, they most often reply, "I don't know; it's just what I do." Because of isolation, humility, and the science of teaching, teachers are often unaware of what it is that makes them successful. Whether you're a leader or teacher, observing and interacting with teachers on a regular basis are powerful ways to begin to discover, develop, and celebrate teachers' unfair advantages.

We work to help students find their passions and strengths, and we ought to be doing the same with our colleagues. Finding your unfair advantage is not about competition but rather an internal sense of confidence and purpose. It speaks to Pink's (2009) and Schwartz's (2015) notion of mastery and autonomy. While teacher satisfaction research can vary, many studies indicate that the lack of autonomy is growing in education (Sparks & Malkus, 2015). If teachers were told to embrace what makes them unique, to find and foster their unfair advantages, I can't help but surmise that it would make a significant difference to job satisfaction. The unfair advantage of schools is the diversity of students and teachers. Having teachers who have varying strengths and personalities should be embraced and encouraged. Instead, too often the desire for consistency has robbed us of the power of diversity. Certainly, it's a delicate balance, but I'd encourage some deeper conversation about how to attain both. Currently, the pendulum falls closer to standardizing teaching than embracing diversity. The fear continues to be that in the name of equity, we have to teach similar things in similar ways. The system's attempt is not to do harm or strip teachers of their autonomy but to ensure all students have an equal opportunity to learn. My contention is that often policies and expectations are emphasized more than teacher autonomy because it's easier to have everyone on the same page of the curriculum than to allow individual teachers to decide what and how to teach based on their students' needs.

Unfair Advantage in Action

The following teachers supported their unfair advantages and thus embraced a culture of joy in their classrooms.

John Einarson was my high school social studies teacher. Many classes would begin with stories of rock and roll in the 1960s. Einarson was an expert in rock-and-roll history and would later go on to write several books on this topic. For a sixteen-year-old kid, this was fascinating stuff. These stories sometimes connected to history and the curriculum, but I most often remember them being an intriguing sidebar to the "real" learning. I don't know if Einarson recognized this as his unfair advantage, but looking back, it certainly was. This is one of my few memories of high school that stands out.

Diana Williams (2013) is an elementary teacher from Surrey, British Columbia. She is a strong advocate for student empowerment. Having spent time in her classroom, it's clear that one of her many unfair advantages is her ability to trust students to do good work. For Williams, this is more than simply a cliché. She uses Kiva, a micro-lending website, to challenge her students to finance small loans to people in third-world countries. Students fundraise through craft sales and other events and then decide who will receive their loans. Tying it to curriculum outcomes, this activity becomes not only highly engaging and relevant to students but also empowering. Students get to make decisions that will deeply impact others' lives.

Joy is something very difficult to achieve when we aren't able to be our true selves. For both students and teachers, that should mean a focus on strengths. Being aware of our weaknesses is important, but far too often, weaknesses dominate our experiences in schools. Finding your unfair advantage is a key ingredient to a truly joyful culture.

Questions to Explore

- Do you see teaching more as a science or an art? Think of ways you are artful in your teaching. What are some research-based ideas you hold to as a teacher?
- What is your unfair advantage? How do you celebrate it?

Chapter 4
A Sense of Wonder

We have a responsibility to awe.

—Jason Silva

When I began teaching first grade, a veteran teacher on staff gave me a copy of Robert Fulghum's (1988) book *All I Really Need to Know I Learned in Kindergarten: Uncommon Thoughts on Common Things*. It served both to inspire and remind me that as a new teacher about to start a career, learning was far less complicated than I thought. While all the ideas in the book are gems worth pondering, the one that struck home was this: "Be aware of wonder. Remember the little seed in the Styrofoam cup: The roots go down and the plant goes up and nobody really knows how or why, but we are all like that" (p. 5).

Walk into most elementary classrooms in springtime, and you'll see these cups lining the window sills. My class was no different. It would be easy to focus solely on the science and explain every aspect of the process. As is often the case, the wonder gets passed over and what should be a beautiful, mysterious occurrence gets *schoolified*. According to Beth Rubin (2012), *schoolified* refers to completing an assignment or project with minimal effort in order to comply and check it off a to-do list. While science is a necessary and powerful element to understand our world, we must always acknowledge wonder. Asking good questions, being curious, and living in wonder are ingredients essential to a culture of joy. The instant access to information and a lack of mindfulness have made appreciating wonder increasingly difficult.

Instant Access to Information

In a world with instant access to information, it's easy to bypass opportunities to wonder. My friend Alec Couros (2012) writes about one such experience with his son.

While grocery shopping, his son asked an interesting question:

> "Do bananas grow with tips up or with tips down?" Since we don't have a lot of banana plants in Regina, I didn't actually know off-hand. But, being the connected father I am, I pulled out my iPhone, Googled it, and in less than 30 seconds, we were looking at photos of banana plants and we no longer had to wonder. *We no longer had to wonder.* (Couros, 2012)

The Internet is a wonderful invention and is a wonder in itself. While we all marvel at the ability to find answers instantaneously, losing our ability to wonder is a dangerous byproduct. Couros's son has a natural, childlike view of the world, and his question represents an attitude and perspective that will bring continued joy if it is fostered and valued.

Remember those friendly arguments and discussions you had with your friends before we had technology at our fingertips? Who played shortstop for the 1983 New York Yankees? What year did *Schindler's List* win best picture at the Academy Awards? While these aren't necessarily wondrous questions, the fact that there was doubt led to recollections, conversations, and even rabbit holes of thought that simply don't happen today because these questions are answered immediately with a simple google.

At the same time, to ignore the access we now have to information as a way to foster a greater sense of wonder is also a mistake. Being able to pull up a video of an animal in nature can trigger great conversations and questions. Using tools like Google Earth or Google Street View to reference an exact location can further curiosity. I rarely watch a movie or documentary without searching Wikipedia or other sources to extend my learning and understanding.

Like Couros, we all need to recognize when we eliminate wonder from our lives. Technology indeed offers many new opportunities to wonder and explore, but our familiarity can rob us of moments when time in thought leads to much more than an answer.

Mindfulness

How often do we forget to see the wonder that exists all around us? We are all guilty of rushing through the day and missing out on the simple moments of beauty and mystery. The idea of stopping to smell the roses is an antiquated concept in a world where being busy is revered and not being busy is associated with laziness and sloth. Most of us refer to our lives almost daily as busy. We want our students to be busy. Free time is a reward for getting your work done. Rarely do we encourage students to slow down and take time to think, breathe, and wonder. The school day is often crammed full of up to eight different class periods with students moving quickly between subjects. Add homework and nonstop after-school activities, and we have pretty much taken away any time for students to simply notice stuff or reflect on things they've seen. Adults and children have become victims to this ridiculous pace, and many are oblivious to its effects on our natural ability to wonder and see the world around us.

We may need to consider strategies for not only coping but thriving and reintroducing wonder to our lives. Having a wondering disposition is indeed part of a joyful life. Being able to not only appreciate but think deeply about nature, literature, history, mathematics, and art is what makes us learners. At its core, mindfulness can be a simple way to provide students with the skills needed to reflect, focus, and calm themselves in a world that is constantly moving and seeking their attention. Mindfulness is getting a fair bit of attention in society and as something that can be deployed in schools. There are numerous programs and supports found online as to how to begin implementing this practice in the classroom.

As a starter, here are some simple ways to incorporate mindfulness into the classroom (see also Davis, 2015, and Stevens, 2016).

- **Begin class with five minutes of journaling:** Simply asking students to reflect in some way on a past experience or personal perspective is a calming and mindful exercise.

- **Introduce breathing exercises:** Breathing exercises, such as those from yoga, can create awareness and calm. Ensure students understand these benefit both their physical and mental health.

- **Just sit there:** Sounds simple, but make it a challenge to see how long your entire class can sit still. Most likely, it will only last a few seconds to start, but collectively reflecting on the challenge may help build stamina. If your entire class can sit still for even a minute, it is a step toward mindfulness.

I commit to mindfulness through photography by taking a photo every day. Encouraged by the work of people like D'Arcy Norman (2007), I decided this would be one way for me to ensure that I pause each day to find something around me that warrants a closer look. While I'm fortunate to travel and see many new things, I also work out of my home, and some days I don't necessarily see things that elicit wonder. Having done this now since 2008, I'm forced to look deeply at items that have become commonplace. It might be seeing the way the light hits glass. Maybe it's imagining what my dog is thinking. Even if it's for a moment, taking a picture is a way to keep myself accountable to a task that I believe leads to mindfulness and wonder. Making this part of my daily routine has been a constant reminder that beauty exists everywhere and is worth noticing and capturing. The simple act of doing mindful activities is indeed an example of mindfulness.

Wonder in Action

The following teachers embrace a culture of joy by incorporating wonder into their classrooms.

Beth Woof (n.d.) is a vice principal in Hamilton, Ontario. Her blog, *FalconPLog* (https://falconplog.wordpress.com), is one of the simplest, most beautiful commitments to wonder. She refers to it as a *plog* (personal learning blog) and uses a formula to focus her writing. She begins with a short paragraph describing some event or experience and then concludes each post with what she's grateful for and what she's curious about (Woof, n.d.). While this is mostly for herself, sharing it publicly is a powerful way to model and build a culture of learning.

Roy Norris (2013) is a high school English teacher in Winnipeg, Manitoba. Every day he drives by grain fields on his way to work. During one of those trips, he wondered, "How much wheat do you need to grow a loaf of bread?" Instead of leaving that thought to float away, he decided to share his question with his family. So with the help of his young daughters, they planted wheat in their backyard to see if indeed they could grow a loaf of bread from scratch. They also created a blog, *Grow a Loaf of Bread* (http://growaloafofbread.blogspot.com), and documented and shared their journey. Each post features photos and a simple reflection on what they did, how they did it, and what they learned. Norris (2013) ends each post with a beautiful sentence: "And that is all we know so far." These words suggest a well-being with accomplishments and a hope that there's more to come. I'm not sure there's a more perfect sentence to describe learning and wonder.

Michelle Baldwin (2014) is a teacher in Colorado who allowed her fourth-grade students to name their class. They chose Architects of Wonder. This name remains as she's transitioned to teaching kindergarten. Students referring to themselves as the Architects of Wonder determines the tone and culture of learning. I've read a lot of mission statements, and very few of them include the word *wonder*. Yet I believe it *is* our mission. Creating and designing opportunities for wonder sets the tone for joyous learning. Expectation, excitement around discovering, and learning make for a welcoming space.

Consider the difference between these examples of wonder in action and what we see in many other classrooms, where graphs showing test results or curriculum standards (disguised by "I can" statements or other subversive methods) trick kids into learning. While I know that statement might seem harsh, I'm questioning the motive behind what we do. These efforts make it seem like we don't find learning all that interesting. Such quantification is also a way to explain every aspect of learning. Embracing wonder means many questions will never get answered. Can there be joy in the unknown? I hope so. While there is much to learn that is known and universal, there is far more that is unknown and worth exploring, if only to appreciate and acknowledge the mysteries. Often these are the very things we avoid because of the nuance and complexity. Not knowing has become an uncomfortable state rather than something humans should embrace.

Perhaps the most important thing we can do in our classrooms to create a greater sense of wonder is to simply value questions more than answers. This is certainly contrary to how we've traditionally viewed schools. Schools are places to learn things, find answers to questions, and leave with knowledge. Questions suggest doubt, uncertainty, and mystery. Yet the idea that we learn to ask really interesting questions is indeed what sustains us and what makes us true learners. Recognizing that "that is all we know so far" means there's more to know. What if instead of emphasizing and celebrating what we know, we encourage students to share what they don't know and want to explore more about? Posing questions, problems, or scenarios is the basis of inquiry learning. Often, inquiry-based learning is an intimidating pedagogy that requires time and effort to properly implement. Perhaps simply getting students to ask more questions is an entry point. Like Beth Woof, prodding students to articulate what they are curious about would send a message that questions are valuable. In fact, avoiding the urge to answer them immediately would serve an important purpose. Having students leave each day with a question would begin the shift to a culture that values knowing to one that values wondering.

Questions to Explore

- What do you wonder about? Have you shared this with your students?
- How can you be more intentional about your personal and professional curiosity?

Chapter 5
Play as Research

The highest form of research is essentially play.
—N. V. Scarfe

In Doug Thomas and John Brown's (2011) *A New Culture of Learning*, the authors make it clear that play is essential in making sense of a world full of new opportunities: "In a world of near-constant flux, play becomes a strategy for embracing change, rather than a way for growing out of it" (p. 48). Play is no longer something only children should experience. Stuart Brown, president of the National Institute for Play, describes play as "anything that spontaneously is done for its own sake" (as cited in Tippett, 2014).

Research suggests that play should remain an integral part of learning, not just in the early years but for life (Caine, 2013; Conklin, 2014). Again, looking to Finland, schools find great success in their early-years programs not by eliminating play but by embracing it. In fact, the article "The Joyful, Illiterate Kindergartners of Finland" examines the playful nature of schools in structured and thoughtful ways designed to expose students to natural, joyful learning opportunities (Walker, 2015). Now when it comes to learning, technology affords us endless opportunities for play. Apps and devices alone give us a chance to try new ideas with low risk. Clay Shirky (2008) notes, "Cheap failure, valuable as it is on its own, is also a key part of a more complex advantage: the exploration of multiple possibilities" (as cited in Sivers, n.d.).

As someone who began teaching in the late 1980s, trying new things in the classroom was complicated. Using new resources or pedagogies required time and expertise that I lacked as a young teacher. I had limited access to materials and new ideas. As I continued my career, emphasis on using research-based ideas and best practices added further caution about venturing into unknown territories.

The advent of the Internet and digital technologies offered a resurgence in my enthusiasm and provided new possibilities for play that I never had previously. Access to ideas and people meant that I was exposed to a plethora of ways to engage my students. Using digital media meant I could supplement my teaching with visuals that took my students to places not possible before. Sites like Discovery Education, YouTube, and Skype added even more means to teach differently. Watching my role shift from instructor to guide and designer was both effective and challenging. When I shared something new with colleagues, I was often met with uncertainty around its value, how difficult it might be to implement, and how it fit with the research. The problem was that for many of the things I was trying, like Skyping in experts or creating videos, there was no research. The best I could do was read what others around the world were doing via personal blogs.

Blogging

While blogging educators were not researchers in the traditional sense, their posts about what worked and what didn't was invaluable to me. Bloggers such as Will Richardson, David Warlick, and Vicki Davis were sharing ideas and opinions that both supported my work and stretched my thinking. My experimentation led to many innovations in my own classroom. When I took on a district position, I continued to connect educators with others by sharing new practices, tools, and ideas. By using free tools such as Blogger and Google Earth, these were fairly low-risk efforts. Soon, teachers I worked with began sharing their new finds and ideas. For some teachers, tools like Blabberize or GeoFlickr were superficial or simply didn't resonate and ended up being discarded quickly, while other ideas like creating classroom wikis and blogs were transformative. Learning is indeed joyful, and for me, this was a new and unchartered way of learning that reinvigorated my career. The ability to connect with people from around the globe quickly and easily was transformative.

The Internet exploded with the advent of blogging. I began my personal blog in 2005. With little knowledge of what blogging was, I signed up for a free account on Blogger. Previously, I had learned HTML and taught teachers how to create webpages to use with students. A handful of teachers in our district seemed interested in improving communication with parents, and we borrowed heavily from an idea of Tony Vincent's, a fifth-grade teacher in Omaha. Vincent had his students provide class updates and summaries of their learning every day on their blog *The Daily Planet* (http://mps.mpsomaha.org/willow/p5/log/log.html). This was a powerful way for classrooms to better connect with parents and explore the Internet. Many teachers adopted this concept, and, using tools like Dreamweaver, the teacher updated these pages as a joint writing activity at the end of each day or week. They then uploaded the page to a web server. It was a fairly steep learning curve combined with an understanding of File Transfer Protocol (FTP).

Blogging had some interesting new potential and eliminated some of the more technical barriers of publishing to the Internet. I offered many workshops in the district on new tools, and blogging was just another tool. One attendee seemed interested in using this with her students. That interest led us to explore what other options she could deploy so all her students could blog. That teacher was Kathy Cassidy (2013), who explored and played with blogging and found great success. Not only were her students writing and communicating more with parents, but the new connections she developed transformed her classroom. She has since gone on to publish a book, *Connected From the Start*, about this experience and other tools that continue to improve learning for her students (Cassidy, 2013).

When I worked in a district as a digital learning consultant, I was charged with creating a technology framework that described our vision on technology and learning. As part of our goals, I used the word *play* to describe the environment and disposition I felt would foster innovation. Like the experience with Cassidy, I noticed that technology was something playful that enabled more than simply incorporating new tools. It was invigorating teachers and students. Unfortunately, senior administration felt the word was not fitting for a formal document. While I was able to articulate the intent, leaders saw *play* as juvenile—certainly not meant for serious learning. I was asked to use another word.

My experience with using new tools and ideas feels a lot like play. The notion of waiting for a whitepaper or research to prove the effectiveness of new technologies makes little sense. Innovation and research can sometimes make for strange bedfellows. By the time research gets to the users, the tools change. With open-source and app development, often the strategy was to give access to users, knowing the product had flaws that would be worked out with feedback. This mindset is somewhat foreign to educators. Textbooks and resources are implemented as gospel. Straying from them isn't generally accepted. In a culture where we value structure, compliance, and order, disruption and uncertainty make for stark contrasts, but we must embrace the possibility for play.

Embracing the Possibility

In 2008, I received an interesting call from Carla Dolman, a teacher in my district. She asked, "What can I do with these cell phones?" She used the word *these* because she didn't own a cell phone but two-thirds of her ninth-grade classroom did. She saw possibility but was looking for some support in seeing if indeed they had potential for learning. At the time, the iPhone wasn't even available in Canada, so the concept of a smartphone was quite new. Viewing mobile phones as learning tools was not only novel, but they generally were viewed as purely a distraction. Signs were posted in most high schools banning their use. And yet Dolman was intrigued. Together, Dolman and I began conversations about what we might do to explore and play with these new tools. We ended up forming a partnership with a local Internet service provider who was equally excited about the potential. In short, SaskTel provided every student with a Blackberry device and a data plan for six months, and we worked with students to develop a plan to use the devices and determine their value for learning. Students and teachers worked in tandem to explore the affordances of mobile technology and document their findings (McCaughan, 2009). While it lacked the structure of formal research, our experimentation provided valuable insight into what worked and what didn't. At the time, little formal research existed on mobile learning. In fact, Liz Kolb from the University of Michigan heard about this initiative and invited students to share their findings via video conferencing (Kolb, 2008; Shareski, 2008). The students also shared their findings at other conferences. Inviting them to play and explore with these technologies led to increased engagement and, I would argue, joy.

Consider the experience of Jared Heidinger (2013), a biology teacher from Lethbridge, Alberta. One night he was flying his toy helicopter around his house and wondered if there was some way he could incorporate this into his classroom. He came up with a crazy idea. Since his students were required each week to learn a set of vocabulary words for their provincial exam, he wondered if he could fly the helicopter around the room like a traffic helicopter and land it on a table. Then, as it landed, he could play a video with someone from another part of the world reading these vocabulary words. The idea seemed awkward and somewhat ridiculous, but this became a highlight for Heidinger and his students. Not only was Heidinger able to be a little silly, but these videos from famous and not-so-famous people around the world made a rather mundane task a little more joyful. Many of the videos were from people he knew or taught, including National Hockey League player Kris Versteeg. Soon, he simply sent out emails to people he thought might be willing to perform this simple task and who also might seem interesting to his students. The creators of *Phineas and Ferb*, national broadcasters, and many more participated. They became part of Heidinger's Homework Chopper series (Heidinger, 2013). While it is so much more efficient to simply give the students the words for the quiz, all this silliness and play had purpose: to make learning more joyful. This was not lost on Heidinger's students, who not only spoke to the fun at the moment but, I dare say, will always remember their biology teacher and even some of the terms (CTV Lethbridge News, 2013).

I suppose some might say these were experiments or explorations, and those words sound more sophisticated than *play*. I disagree. *Play* is indeed intentional here because, unlike experimentation or exploration, it suggests that active engagement is the essential component and that end results are welcomed but not necessarily the focus. That's not to say results aren't important, but they only happen because there are dozens of other times when new tools were tried with little or no positive results. Experimentation, while useful, suggests a more rigid approach that also can be intimidating to many. When you invite folks to play with ideas, tools, and scenarios, it immediately takes the pressure off failure as the end to learning. Instead, failure becomes accepted as an element to learning and growing. Classroom teachers, and in fact all learners, need time to experiment with clearly defined outcomes and purposes but also time to play with less emphasis on results. Both are learning pedagogies. Play leads to innovation, which is certainly highly sought after in this age. It is indeed a joyful word that students and educators alike can embrace. Let's not be afraid to use it.

Questions to Explore

- What does play look like to you? What does play look like in your school or classroom?
- How can you use play to foster new and innovative ideas for your school or district?

Chapter 6
A Sense of Community

We have a classroom system when we could have a community system.

—Deborah Baker

It's been argued that all learning is social. Whether face to face, via conversations with people in the same room, or by reading an author's work, learning is something that involves other people. However, schools were not designed to be social spaces. Schools were designed for efficiency. Classrooms were simply a way to bring large numbers of children together and disseminate information with the hope of them acquiring knowledge at the same time. As a student growing up in the 1970s and 1980s, I didn't think of school as a community. I found community and care from my family and friends and institutions like churches and clubs. I had no expectation that school was anything more than a rite of passage to adulthood. As young children and teenagers, we naturally seek to socialize in school but know the protocol remains: keep your eyes on your own paper, don't talk, and do as you're told. Socialization was something that was at best tolerated and at worst prohibited under strict supervision and rules. As sterile and antiquated as that might seem to some, it remains a fairly accurate description of many modern-day schools.

The Importance of Community

The late Grant Wiggins (2014) shares a powerful story of a veteran-teacher-turned coach, who decided to shadow a couple of high school students for two days. The teacher's findings, while obviously anecdotal, are telling. She shares three key takeaways. (The anonymous teacher was later revealed to be Wiggins's daughter Alexis.)

1. Students sit a lot, and it's exhausting to them.

2. Students' days are 90 percent listening.

3. Students and teachers feel like a nuisance.

These findings are not likely surprising. The last finding resonated with me. The idea of feeling like a nuisance in your own school suggests it's not really your school but someone else's. When a teacher walks into someone else's classroom or space, the assumption is that it does not belong to him or her. Students might feel some connection to their classmates, but unless someone invites them to have a say beyond accounting for their learning, they're in a classroom, not a community.

As we recognize that one cannot separate the emotional and social from the academic, things are changing. There is a concerted effort to address the needs of the whole child. However, this effort still focuses on the individual. Intentionally creating community is not a universal goal for all schools.

Few educators would say they don't believe in creating a sense of community, but if you, like the shadowing teacher, took inventory of the language you hear most often, you might be surprised. Phrases like "mind your own business," "keep your eyes on your own work," and "no talking" are uttered regularly in most schools. Certainly, they aren't meant to demean and are sometimes necessary. But in far too many cases, this represents the dominant language and perception of schools and classrooms. Students are sent clear messages that being together with others in a room is not only unimportant but often a detriment and a distraction to learning. The way many teach would work best if students were in sound-proof cubicles wearing blinders, with only the voice of the teacher audible. While that is hyperbole, I'm not sure it's that far from the way students feel. Classrooms are often about control, compliance, and order. Communities are about a shared purpose and belonging. Joy is about contentment and a sense of well-being. Joy is the opportunity and power of living and learning in community.

It's pretty hard to deny that we're living in the best possible time to be a learner. Access to information and experts allows for unprecedented learning opportunities. At the same time, it is probably the most challenging time for schools because they realize that selling facts is a dying business. In chapter 3, I talked about educators finding their unfair advantages. When it comes to school, they indeed have an unfair advantage in today's learning environment but for the most part are ignoring it. The unfair advantage of schools is that every morning, a bus drops students off at the door. This is a unique opportunity to bring together a large, diverse group of humans who are developing and need the nurturance, wisdom, and care of adults and each other. Unfortunately, too often we're ignoring this great gift.

I'm not sure which comes first—joyful learning or community—but it's just about impossible to have one without the other. When students feel like they are part of a community, joy is possible. When students, like teachers, perceive school as someone else's space, they feel like a nuisance—survival is based on complying to someone's rules. A simple, but useful, litmus test is how teachers describe their learning space. Do teachers refer to "my classroom" or to "our classroom"? Calling it "our classroom" invites students to be part of it. Taking that a step further by asking for and implementing student feedback creates a greater sense of community. If instead teachers talk about "my classroom" and "my rules," the chances of community to emerge is almost zero. Communities are not about authority and rules but rather a shared experience:

> The journey begins as we share our stories, be they stories of fears or of joy. Sharing helps us to open up, to become vulnerable, to hear other people's stories. Thus do we begin to work together to distinguish truth from untruth and rational fear from irrational fear, to determine what we might do together. When we really hear one another, the bond of community is forged between us. We smile at each other; we feel warmth and joy as if we are home. (Born, 2014, p. 207)

Certainly, creating community doesn't mean zero rules or authority; rather it's about emphasis.

Community Over Convenience

In 2007, I began teaching online. Online instruction at the time was largely a digital version of traditional correspondence courses. At the postsecondary level, students' primary reason for taking online courses was convenience. Being able to study from a distance and without the constraints of time meant they didn't have to disrupt other opportunities to further their education. Two months before my course began, I received an email from a student asking if I could send her all the assignments ahead of time. I assumed she had taken online courses before and wanted to work ahead so that when the course opened she could submit all her work and be done. While this was a reasonable request, it forced me to ask myself an important question: "What role do community and social learning play in my course?" I had to tell her that while I understood that many online courses allow for asynchronous deadlines, it wouldn't work for mine.

I made a conscious decision from that point that I wasn't interested in offering a course that emphasized convenience over community. That might make sense for some types of learning, but the affordance of digital technology means we can overcome barriers of time and space to connect students with each other and also with learners beyond the course. However, this is no different for face-to-face situations, be it a kindergarten class or a high school mathematics course. If the "mind your own business" mindset rules, student interaction and collaboration become an event at best.

Dave Cormier's (2008) great work on rhizomatic learning suggests that the community is the curriculum. That's a jolting statement to many, but ignoring this in a connected world is naive:

> What is needed is a model of knowledge acquisition that accounts for socially constructed, negotiated knowledge. In such a model, the community is not the path to understanding or accessing the curriculum; rather, *the community is the curriculum*. (Cormier, 2008; emphasis added)

While I certainly didn't have the full background and depth of understanding that Cormier and others had, I knew from my own experiences that unless I made an effort to connect my students with each other and those outside the course, I would be robbing them of what I believe is an essential skill and disposition of a 21st century learner. At this point I wasn't sure what specific things I would do to make this a reality; I just knew I had to make a clear stance that learning as a community was going to be intentional.

Intentional Communities

Think about the communities in which you participate. In some cases, they are based on geography, and in other cases, you've chosen to take part based on your interests and passions. In both instances, well-functioning communities offer a number of ways to contribute. Members have different skills and interests that make the community operate well. People are there for similar reasons, but diversity is what makes it interesting. Schools are a fascinating blend of these two scenarios. Most students attend based on geography, and yet without some invitation to explore and use their passions and interests with one another, it's not likely to feel like a community.

Besides simply calling it "our classroom" or "our school," how can we intentionally create communities instead of classrooms and schools? Perhaps we're closer than we think. There are many things we do each day that create a greater sense of community, but we lack the cumulative impact of doing these things consistently and intentionally, both locally and globally. Communities do happen in some classrooms and schools, but, like many good things, are mostly occurring in pockets. But simple things like smiling at every student as he or she enters the classroom, allowing students to help generate classroom rules, or allowing them to help design the learning space are all ways to establish a community of learners (Schaps, 2005).

Having now taught online for over eight years, the notion of intentionally building community has been a challenge. I fully acknowledge that the limitations of time and space are real. I think, for high schools, time is a limitation that educators have to address. Elementary schools do have the luxury of being able to build deeper relationships simply because students are often together for longer periods of time and sometimes have fewer constraints around scheduling and curriculum. While this may be true, it doesn't guarantee that community will happen. At the same time, the limitations of high school or online courses can move toward more community experiences. In my time as an online instructor, I've made many intentional efforts to create community. While I used them in postsecondary education, teachers could easily modify them for nearly every grade level. Here are a few that are appropriate for all students.

- **Introductory videos:** Each student creates a one- to two-minute introductory video using a smartphone, iPad, or laptop. Even in face-to-face environments, communities have to know one another. The power of creating these "About Me" videos digitally is that they are easily shared either publicly to sites like YouTube or to a district learning management system. Student videos can be shot at home or outside, which allows students to share some of their passions beyond the course. Younger students could easily shoot a few minutes of themselves at home to share with the rest of the class. Think of this as an amplified version of show-and-tell. Older students could use it to share a passion or something they're proud of. Adding a few constraints, and yet keeping it simple, is an invitation to connect beyond what happens in class.

- **Student feedback:** Teachers primarily give feedback, and students expect this of their teacher. However, not only is student-to-student feedback important but so is student-teacher feedback on the instruction and environment. After each assignment, students can submit their own grade and reflections. They can also provide feedback to teachers on how they might improve the unit and assignment. When I use this strategy, it is invaluable. Students have great insight and perspective. The byproduct is that students feel valued and a part of the course.

- **Blogging:** Students can share openly and publicly via blogs. Sites like Blogger, Kidblog, and Weebly are all simply tools to use as a blog and learning portfolio. Transparent sharing helps students own their learning. The idea of a *walled garden* (a website restricted to subscribers) can be a useful starting point, but learning will be limited. Students can delete their work or make it private after, but during the course, they should share their learning with others in their class, and it's even better if it can be made public. This suggests all learning is valuable and that learning from each other is as well. I had one student tell me she felt closer to her classmates in our online course than she did with the courses she was taking face to face. If students never get to see their classmates' work, your chances of creating a community are small. This is a great case for blended learning. Online spaces solve this problem, allowing sharing and access beyond classroom hours and walls. Teachers have a responsibility to protect students from feeling embarrassed or ridiculed by their work. I trust teachers to make this call. However, sharing and discussing student work provides a great opportunity for feedback and, in turn, community.

- **Clear expectations of community:** Many students believe that all knowledge comes from the teacher. At the onset of all my courses, I let my students know this will not be the case. In fact, I let them know they'll be responsible for answering two questions at the end of the course.

  a.   What did you learn from others?

  b.   What did you contribute to others' learning?

  I believe that every classroom, in every grade, could use these two questions as a foundation of community. It lets students know that paying attention to each other will be beneficial and important to their learning. It also suggests that simply taking a course or showing up every day without making a contribution is unacceptable.

I continue to invite students to explore various means and methods that are comfortable and build on their strengths. Online spaces make sharing easy. Students could share interesting articles, videos, and images that connect to content. We have to find many ways students can contribute to the community, particularly for those who are less confident and more introverted. I recall one student asking, "How will I contribute to others' learning? The reason I'm taking this course is because I don't know much." I responded, "One of the best ways to contribute is to ask questions. If you pose a question and allow others to respond, you do two things: you're likely asking a question others were afraid to ask, and you're giving your classmates an opportunity to contribute and share their learning." That to me is the essence of a classroom community. But how does community look in a larger setting, such as a whole school?

School Community

Of course, the notion of community extends well beyond the classroom. In fact, when we associate the word *community* with schools, we likely think of parents and other interested folks who may not be students. These are also part of the idea of community that when nurtured and honored leads to more joyful learners. There are some great examples of leaders, particularly principals, who actively and intentionally foster and build community. I reached out to my network via Twitter to ask how educators foster community in their classroom, school, or district (Shareski, 2015).

One of those who responded was Curt Rees. Rees is the principal at Northern Hills Elementary in Onalaska, Wisconsin. He's been very intentional about building and fostering community within his school:

> My teachers are great about building community among the students. Each class has a buddy class of older or younger students and they get together at least once a month to do an activity that requires them to work together.
>
> We also make sure we are having fun and make sure other people know we are having fun. We use our social media accounts to help with this. By looking at our Facebook page and YouTube channel, one will see photos and videos of important community building events that happen within our school. I've learned a lot from Tim Lauer on how to do this. He said too often our schools are black boxes where no one really knows that happens within them. Use social media as a giant window into our schools so parents and the community can see all the good that happens in our schools. (as cited in Shareski, 2015)

Rees is a wonderful example of a leader who sees community not as a concept that just happens but as a result of intention. Speaking of intention, Rees references social media. It's definitely a powerful communication tool, but its use varies. For many, it's simply another way to distribute newsletter items and information. But for those like Rees and Tim Lauer, social media is a clear way to showcase learning and, more specifically, joyful learning. You can't help but look at the images and videos from leaders like this and not think about joy. Educators who use it effectively share photos and videos showing groups of students, student work, and lots and lots of smiles. The message is clear: "We love learning, and we love learning together." Leadership plays a critical role in establishing this joyous culture. For a teacher, principal, or district leader, the accumulation of these messages creates culture. Leisa Reichelt (2007) calls it *ambient intimacy*: "being able to keep in touch with people with a level of regularity and intimacy that you wouldn't usually have access to, because time and space conspire to make it impossible."

Communities aren't perfect, and they don't always work or happen the way we might like. Members aren't always engaged; they don't always treat each other well.

It's not as idyllic as we sometimes envision. But communities are inviting. Communities provide an opportunity to contribute and find meaning with others, and they honor the social experience. Think about your best memories of school. Are they about the time you spent learning in isolation, or are they about things you did with others? Too often the most powerful social experiences of school are left to extracurricular activities. What a shame. Learning together should be prized and nurtured. While it does happen, in too many cases it's either an exception or it just hasn't been acknowledged as necessary. Even as I consider my own teaching practice, I'm constantly examining my design to increase the ideas of community and care. It's a worthy pursuit that when achieved is a joyful, enduring experience.

Questions to Explore

- What happens when your school is seen as a community as opposed to simply an education institution? What benefits arise?
- What challenges might you face when shifting from a classroom to a community?

Chapter 7
Gratitude

Gratitude can transform common days into thanksgivings, turn routine jobs into joy and change ordinary opportunities into blessings.

—William Arthur Ward

You can't really talk about joy without talking about gratitude. It's a chicken and egg thing. Joy might be something you experience and live, but it will flourish when you partner it with gratitude. Once again, this is not a revolutionary idea. It's not something we don't already know intuitively. But I don't know of another profession that does so many wonderful things each day without getting the deserved gratitude. Why is that? I think it begins with how many of us choose the profession.

Teaching Without Receiving Gratitude

We all know going in that we aren't going to get rich being a teacher. Many opt out of high-paying jobs because we want to pursue something honorable. Teaching is a high calling indeed. Because of the real or perceived sacrifice, the educator's mantra becomes, "I don't do this for the money." Educators take most of their satisfaction from the intrinsic motivation of doing meaningful work. Since most educators believe this about themselves and each other, it's easy for them to ignore the need to show outward displays of thanks "because it's just what we do." However, the impact of receiving heartfelt gratitude cannot be understated.

In 2012, I left my job in public education and went to work for Discovery Education. Having spent twenty-three years working in schools, moving to the corporate world was shocking in many respects. One glaring difference was the way in which thanks and gratitude are offered and valued. In my first week of work, my new coworkers showered me with words of encouragement and excitement. I wondered if this was merely something done as part of initiation, but after four

43

years I know it's truly part of the company's DNA. I don't know if every company operates this way, but I've been careful to observe that gratitude is something I didn't experience nearly as regularly as I do now. In turn, I'm much more aware of giving it out, and I realize now more than ever how little teachers and schools receive and distribute gratitude.

I get to speak to thousands of people each year, and I receive an inordinate amount of praise for simply doing my job. I'm not sure what it is—maybe because I'm a guest and they want to be extra hospitable?—but people are so kind with their words. The words of thanks not only make me proud of what I do but also make me want to continue improving. I wish all educators could experience what I experience regularly. The truth is, what teachers do in a classroom is far more taxing than speaking to an audience of adults. Each one deserves to be thanked regularly. Gratitude shouldn't be doled out to incentivize and motivate but given because it's the right thing to do. Gratitude can indeed be a great motivator.

Of course this is so true for our students and classrooms as well. How often are we thankful for our students and do we extend gratitude toward them? This might seem like an odd question. We're providing a service to them. They should be the ones who are thankful. But if we do believe in the role of community, then their contributions and even their presence should be viewed as things to be grateful for. In the purest sense, they are the only reason educators have a job. Imagine for a moment that every day a teacher received a genuine bit of gratitude from a colleague, boss, parent, or student. What difference would that make in his or her job satisfaction? I'm guessing teachers can recall exactly those moments when someone took time to thank them. Now, imagine if a teacher or leader offered that to students or coworkers. What would that do for them? What would that do for the teacher or leader?

Showing Gratitude

In the spring of 2012, I was helping my wife in her classroom and saw a note pinned to her cupboard. It read, "Thank you so much for helping Josh with his tooth yesterday. Keeping it secure for the tooth fairy's visit last night was very important to him. Have a great day!"

If you've taught primary students, you know that putting a tooth in a ziplock bag is not unusual. What was unusual was receiving a thank-you note from a grandparent for this tiny act of kindness. The grandmother wrote the note in September. I visited the class in April. The note stayed there for eight months because it reminded my wife that what she does matters. Even these little noncurricular duties matter. For the grandparent, writing the note wasn't likely a major effort. For my wife, however, receiving that note represented why she does what she does.

As mentioned, it's also important to show our thanks to students. Zac Chase (2011), a former high school teacher, uses high-grade compliments (HGCs), choosing one student in each class to compliment. A high-grade compliment has three components: (1) be in close proximity, (2) make eye contact, and (3) be thoughtful. Really think about what makes that person unique and valued. It's beyond surface-level appreciation of the student's specific character or behaviors.

Chase shares a story on his blog about Sam, a student who wanted to give a high-grade compliment to another student:

> Sam was out of her seat and positioning herself in front of Douglas. As shocked as everyone else in the class was of her placement, no one was more shocked than Douglas.
>
> Douglas and Sam are any kind of oil-and-water-esque metaphor you can think of. They bicker, they tease, they call each other names.
>
> And Sam was about to give him a HGC.
>
> I was maybe holding my breath.
>
> "Even though we call each other names and pick on each other, that's just how we do. That's Sam and Douglas," she began.
>
> "I wouldn't want it any different. You're like a brother to me. I know if there's any part of the homework that I don't understand, I can come to you and you'll put the kidding aside and help me. And I know, when something's wrong with you, you know you can come to me and I'll try to help you. So, even though we call each other names and fight all the time, I wouldn't want it any other way. 'Cause then we wouldn't be Sam and Douglas."
>
> And then the class applauded. (Chase, 2011)

Many would find this an uncomfortable, perhaps unnecessary, bit of interaction, but gratitude needs to be modeled and in some cases explicitly taught. A simple, but thoughtful, ritual like this provides great learning, motivation, validation, and acceptance that many students and adults desperately need. Joy thrives as people feel accepted and appreciated.

I've been trying to be better at showing gratitude. During the holiday season of 2015, I wanted to offer a fun way to say thank you to some of the people in my personal learning network. Scanning through my Twitter feed, I decided to have a little fun and created arbitrary awards. I called them the #deanies. I simply began offering random, and somewhat silly, bits of thanks to a number of my friends and associates. My intent was to pause and think about what connected us. Sometimes it was a shared memory, and other times it was a trait or accomplishment of theirs. I was somewhat taken aback by how many people took great satisfaction in my 140-character bit of gratitude. Yet I'm constantly reminded how many times teachers and students go through days, and maybe even weeks, without ever really being thanked. That's appalling.

Certainly there are many other ways to demonstrate thanks and gratitude. It might mean you'll need to schedule it and do something proactive as part of your day. Handwritten notes and cards are excellent tools for gratitude. Phone calls and conversations are also effective. Text messages, tweets, emails, and blog comments are all simple ways to let folks know they matter and that they do good work. This is a wake-up call for everyone, including me, to be better at offering gratitude.

I work with districts that have lofty initiatives to improve and transform learning. Many of these initiatives involve detailed plans and strategies designed to bring about success. Smart people spend a great deal of time ensuring their goals are met. Usually there are high demands and expectations placed on classroom teachers to lead, but have you built in times to celebrate and be grateful? I'm not talking about an *end of the year, when and if we meet our goals* kind of celebration but rather something that happens on a regular basis. I'm confident that if educators doubled the amount of gratitude they offer, any initiative in the classroom, school, or district would be greatly enhanced and would significantly increase their chances of success. But beyond its role to see success, gratitude is an essential ingredient for a joyful culture and life.

Questions to Explore

- Think of a time when you received gratitude. What impact did that have beyond just making you feel good?
- How can you make gratitude a seamless part of your day? How could you use technology to support this?

Conclusion

What avail is it to win prescribed amounts of information about geography and history, to win the ability to read and write, if in the process the individual loses his own soul?

—John Dewey

I hope you've figured out there isn't a recipe for joy. There are indeed elements that make for joyful learning, but there is no step-by-step manual. Some of you may have identified current practices that should be labeled as joyful. That's fantastic. I encourage you to build on and share those. However, others are looking for somewhere to begin. My only advice is to *just go for it.*

Most of us working in education will agree we have a tremendously difficult job. The demands from leaders, policymakers, businesses, community members, parents, and students can be overwhelming. Most teachers put additional pressure on themselves to be great. Educators are pulled in every direction, and the sense that the work is never done lingers. In turn, they pass this stress and pressure along to students. I fully recognize the complexity of our roles. If at any point I seemed to simplify or ignore this, that was never my intent. Report cards are still being written. Standardized tests are being given. Bells ring every day. There are many things about our day-to-day lives that just have to get done, and it's difficult to see where joy lives in these tasks. That said, my goal is to push your thinking. If you're still saying, "Yeah, but . . . ," that's okay. I don't have it all figured out. This book is meant to create a conversation about what needs to be talked about a whole lot more. I'm hoping I've either affirmed, convinced, or at least provoked you regarding the concept of joy and its role in our schools.

It's always useful to have some practical examples or direct responses from other educators. I reached out on Twitter to see what other educators did that was purely for joy (Shareski, 2015b). I received some great ideas that you might consider doing with your classroom, school, or district (see Shareski, n.d., for all the responses).

Michelle Hiebert, a kindergarten teacher from British Columbia:

Every day, no matter what else is going on, my class takes time to read by the "fire" (a video of the TV fireplace). The students get cozy on the carpet, huddle in close around me, and I read to them. It is our absolute favorite time of the day. I also have other locations to choose from (the beach, a babbling brook) . . . or best of all, we go outside to sit under a big tree in the corner of our playground and read together. I'm not sure which is more joyful . . . the reading, or the being together.

Even my most challenging students love this daily ritual. My non-verbal student with autism cuddles in close. My fidgety, active students listen in rapt attention. Everyone has this look of bliss on their little faces as they listen to me read to them.

Matt Miller, a grade 6 teacher from Indiana:

I use my guitar in class a lot. I'll do announcements and/or instructions in song. The best is when I take it into the hallway during passing periods and "serenade" students as they walk by singing made-up songs. Also, test reminder songs during passing periods work great as well.

Typically, the goofier the better. When you make students smile, it's a better day.

Kat Ling, a grade 7 teacher from British Columbia:

We have dance parties—sometimes in class, sometimes after school. My kids love to dance. We also have *Just Dance* contests. The kids are on different sides of the room and I project a *Just Dance* video using YouTube. I give points for singing nicely, best overall group performance, top 3 individual performances.

I had boys who stayed till I kicked them out at 4:30 on the last day of school before winter break. They were dancing and smiling the whole time. Even my boy who broke his leg, was dancing in his boot cast.

Ken Olsen, a dean of students from Indiana:

Staff has a weekly theme dress day on Thursdays just for the fun of it, plus a monthly night out for an activity (bowling, trivia night, see *Star Wars* on opening night).

I believe it has brought staff closer together.

Chris Kennedy, a superintendent from British Columbia:

Each year during the week before Christmas our entire Executive Team loads up our sleigh and visits every classroom delivering a cookie to each staff member. One year we were Santa and his elves, another year we wore our tacky Christmas sweaters and this year we wore our Christmas pajamas.

It is great and people are expecting us now and wondering when we will come and what we will wear—it helps build community. One teacher said to me "It is the second last day before Christmas break, I was worried you guys weren't coming this year." Another teacher said, "Now I have something to dream about tonight—our leaders in their pajamas."

Tom Glennon, a principal from Delaware:

I wear a different pair of fun/crazy socks to work every day. That's it. Very easy. But the students absolutely love it! It has helped me build relationships with students and makes me much more approachable.

Through my sock obsession, I've been able to encourage students and staff to help others through socks . . . sounds weird, I know. :-) Last year (and again this spring) we participated in the "Rock your Socks" campaign to raise awareness for Down Syndrome. We also participated in Kid President's Socktober event and collected 1577 pairs of socks for a local shelter. We capped off this drive with a Socktoberfest at school where everyone wore fun socks.

From a teacher/parent last year:

Thank you Tom!!! My son in 5th grade mentioned you had some dinosaur socks on the other day when you were visiting his classroom. It made his day!!!

Peggy Weber, a principal from Florida:

As a way of reinforcing positive hallway behavior, when I come upon a group of children patiently waiting for their teacher in the hall, I "steal them." While the teacher is pre-occupied with their task in the office, I have the kids quickly and quietly follow me to a nearby classroom or around the corner. We wait for their teacher to find them missing when he/she comes out of the office, and then enjoy a moment of joy when he/she finds us. I congratulate them on patiently waiting, and tell them I only "steal" classes who are doing things "The Chieftain Way." They love it and remember the time the principal "stole" their class and played a trick on their teacher, and it provides a moment of fun and joyful giggling.

Jen Deyenberg, a director of instruction from Alberta:

On the first professional development day of the school year we have a Rally Day where all staff comes together. Instead of boring speeches we have a day focused on staff wellness. We partner with Alberta Health to offer sessions staff can choose from ranging from canoeing, yoga and Tai Chi, to websites to support wellness, making jam, knitting, and financial planning. We focus on all areas of wellness—spiritual, physical, emotional, financial, intellectual and environmental to increase the quality of occupational wellness.

Many of these ideas are so simple and yet so powerful. They all have a specific intention—embracing a culture of joy. But when a culture is solely focused on things like data and student achievement, these kinds of activities are often filed under "nice but unnecessary" and sometimes considered wasteful. However, taking breaks and engaging in playful, even goofy, activities are useful in learning (Seppala, 2016). Intuitively, we know taking breaks from our routine is healthy and fosters creativity. If these activities involve physical exertion, even better. The lack of movement in many of our schools is alarming. So perhaps using this as your justification might be something to consider.

So many of the expectations in education suggest these types of actions to be frivolous and distracting from the real business of learning. Many teachers wouldn't even think to dive into these kinds of activities for fear of judgment or reprimand, pressure from the district, or personal beliefs that these have no place in an academic institution. But choosing not to engage in acts of joy will also define your culture.

Additionally, in an education environment obsessed with data, these ideas might resonate but also seem difficult to justify. The benefits don't necessarily result in hard data. As difficult as engagement is to measure, joy and contentment are equally as challenging. However, just because something is hard to measure doesn't mean it is unimportant. You may have heard the saying, "We value what we measure, and we measure what we value." This is hardly a universal truth. I value the love I have for my family. That's not easy to measure at all. However, it's evident through words and actions. Even less abstract loves like my love of golf aren't easily measured despite the link to a quantifiable score. My success isn't based solely on a score. It includes the serenity of being in a beautiful environment, time spent with friends, the sunshine, and more. I don't know how to measure all of that and don't need to. Without doing joyful things for joy's sake, we risk creating an environment that perpetuates the notion that schools are hyperserious business and that taking time to do things unrelated to data undermines student achievement. We've got to come to terms with this, but sometimes waiting for permission means it's too late.

There's no recipe for joy, but the ideas I've shared may get you started or boost you in your current journey. Learning should be about beauty, wonder, and curiosity. Learning is a social, participatory experience. Those two sentences alone can't help but conjure up images of joy.

No matter what role you play—teacher, leader, student, parent, or curious human—joy requires intention, and it needs to be shared. My hope is that even a few of you will do this and let me know if joy has indeed been a worthy pursuit. I think I know the answer but would still love to hear about it.

Questions to Explore

- What joyful acts have you performed lately? Are there ones you've done for any purpose in particular?
- How do you measure the well-being of your school or classroom?

References and Resources

Aderhold, D. M. (2016). *Letter to the community from Dr. David Aderhold, superintendent of schools*. Accessed at www.west-windsor-plainsboro.k12.nj.us /common/pages/DisplayFile.aspx?itemId=30680884 on May 5, 2016.

Azzam, A. M. (2007). Special report: Why students drop out. *Educational Leadership, 64*(7), 91–93. Accessed at www.ascd.org/publications/educational-leadership /apr07/vol64/num07/Why-Students-Drop-Out.aspx on January 3, 2015.

Baldwin, M. (2014). *About Team Baldwin*. Accessed at https://architectsofwonder .edublogs.org/about-team-baldwin on January 29, 2016.

Born, P. (2014). *Deepening community: Finding joy together in chaotic times*. San Francisco: Berrett-Koehler.

Busteed, B. (2013, January 7). *The school cliff: Student engagement drops with each school year* [Blog post]. Accessed at www.gallup.com/opinion/gallup/170525 /school-cliff-student-engagement-drops-school-year.aspx on October 10, 2014.

Caine, G. (2013). *The power of play for learners of all ages*. Accessed at www .cainelearning.com/the-power-of-play-for-learners-of-all-ages on July 21, 2016.

Cassidy, K. (2013). *Connected from the start: Global learning in the primary grades*. Virginia Beach, VA: Powerful Learning Press.

Charbonneau, J. [JeffCharbonneau]. (2014, October 21). *Relationships then content. Both matter. So does the order. #edchat #edu* [Tweet]. Accessed at https://twitter .com/jeffcharbonneau/status/524738329737437184 on January 25, 2016.

Chase, Z. A. (2011, February 14). *Things I know 44 of 365: Positivity can be viral* [Blog post]. Accessed at www.autodizactic.com/things-i-know-44-of-365 -positivity-can-be-viral on February 1, 2016.

Conklin, H. G. (2014). Toward more joyful learning: Integrating play into frameworks of middle grades teaching. *American Educational Research Journal, 51*(6), 1227–1255.

Cormier, D. (2008, June 3). *Rhizomatic education: Community as curriculum* [Blog post]. Accessed at http://davecormier.com/edblog/2008/06/03/rhizomatic -education-community-as-curriculum on January 31, 2016.

Couros, A. (2012, November 18). *Tips up or tips down?* [Blog post]. Accessed at http://educationaltechnology.ca/couros/2287 on May 5, 2016.

CTV Lethbridge News. (2013, February 7). *Homework chopper!* [Video file]. Accessed at www.youtube.com/watch?v=F2OA0xCQY3E on February 1, 2016.

Downes, S. (2010). A world of change. *The Huffington Post.* Accessed at www.huffingtonpost.com/stephen-downes/a-world-to-change_b_762738.html on July 16, 2016.

Elmore, R. F. (2000). *Building a new structure for school leadership.* Accessed at www.shankerinstitute.org/sites/shanker/files/building.pdf on July 12, 2016.

Elmore, R. F. (2002). *Bridging the gap between standards and achievement.* Accessed at www.shankerinstitute.org/sites/shanker/files/Bridging_Gap.pdf on July 25, 2016.

Feloni, R. (2014, September 10). Here's how a billionaire investor coached an entrepreneur through the pitch process. *Business Insider.* Accessed at www.businessinsider.com/investor-chris-sacca-how-to-pitch-business-2014-9 on January 27, 2016.

Ferriter, B. [plugusin]. (2015, February 15). *Would visitors to your school walk away convinced that learning is an inherently joyful act worthy of celebration? #worthasking #cpchat* [Tweet]. Accessed at https://twitter.com/plugusin/status/566625910213070850 on May 25, 2016.

Floyda007. (2008, May 15). *Learning to change—changing to learn* [Video file]. Accessed at www.youtube.com/watch?v=tahTKdEUAPk on January 31, 2016.

Fulghum, R. (1988). *All I really need to know I learned in kindergarten: Uncommon thoughts on common things.* New York: Villard Books.

Heidinger, J. [Jared Heidinger]. (2013, February 21). *Jared's weekend homework chopper: Kris Versteeg edition* [Video file]. Accessed at www.youtube.com/watch?v=iZWclbg3Afg&list=PLPTIy3JA29L63RQOYFV_ZtoSUXhO1Hs4v on February 1, 2016.

Hsieh, T. (2009, January 3). *Your culture is your brand* [Blog post]. Accessed at www.zappos.com/blogs/your-culture-is-your-brand on January 25, 2016.

Hursh, D. (2001). *Neoliberalism and the control of teachers, students, and learning: The rise of standards, standardization, and accountability.* Accessed at http://clogic.eserver.org/4-1/hursh.html on July 25, 2016.

Jain, R. (2015). *Can stress help students?* Accessed at www.edutopia.org/blog/can-stress-help-students-renee-jain on July 25, 2016.

Joy. (n.d.). In *Merriam-Webster Online Dictionary.* Accessed at www.merriam-webster.com/dictionary/joy on May 5, 2016.

Kohn, A. (2004). Feel-bad education: The cult of rigor and the loss of joy. *Education Week, 24*(3), 36, 44. Accessed at www.edweek.org/ew/articles/2004/09/15/03kohn.h24.html on January 27, 2016.

Kolb, L. (2008). *Inspiration! Bravo to Craik School in Craik, SK.* Accessed at http://
cellphonesinlearning.blogspot.com/2008/06/inspiration-bravo-to-craik-school-in
.html on July 25, 2016.

Lear, L. (2007). *Beatrix Potter: A life in nature.* New York: St. Martin's Press.

Lemann, N. (2013). *How Michelle Rhee misled education reform.* Accessed at https://
newrepublic.com/article/113096/how-michelle-rhee-misled-education-reform on
July 13, 2016.

Leonard, N. R., Gwadz, M. V., Ritchie, A., Linick, J. L., Cleland, C. M., Elliott, L.,
et al. (2015). A multi-method exploratory study of stress, coping, and substance
use among high school youth in private schools. *Frontiers in Psychology, 6.*
Accessed at www.ncbi.nlm.nih.gov/pmc/articles/PMC4511824 on January 27,
2016.

Lulla, M. (2015, September 8). WRSD pays attention to staff wellness. *Drayton Valley
Western Review.* Accessed at www.draytonvalleywesternreview.com/2015/09/08
/wrsd-pays-attention-to-staff-wellness on January 25, 2016.

McCaughan, D. (2009, June 9). *Teach cell phones, don't ban them.* Accessed at www
.knoxnews.com/news/education/teach-cell-phones-dont-ban-them-ep
-409957592-359367751.html on January 31, 2016.

McLeod, S. (2014, December 22). We need schools to be different. *The Huffington
Post.* Accessed at www.huffingtonpost.com/scott-mcleod/we-need-schools-to-be
-dif_b_6353198.html on June 28, 2016.

Newport, C. (2011, November 11). *If you're busy, you're doing something wrong:
The surprisingly relaxed lives of elite achievers* [Blog post]. Accessed at http://
calnewport.com/blog/2011/11/11/if-youre-busy-youre-doing-something-wrong
-the-surprisingly-relaxed-lives-of-elite-achievers on January 25, 2016.

Norman, D. (2007, July 2). *365 photos: Halfway point* [Blog post]. Accessed at https://
darcynorman.net/2007/07/02/365-photos-halfway-point on January 29, 2016.

Norris, R. (2013, October 18). *We grew TWO loaves of bread!* [Blog post]. Accessed at
http://growaloafofbread.blogspot.com/2013/10/we-grew-two-loaves-of-bread
.html on January 29, 2016.

Partanen, A. (2011, December 29). What Americans keep ignoring about Finland's
school success. *The Atlantic.* Accessed at www.theatlantic.com/national/archive
/2011/12/what-americans-keep-ignoring-about-finlands-school-success/250564
on May 5, 2016.

Pink, D. H. (2009). *Drive: The surprising truth about what motivates us.* New York:
Riverhead Books.

Positive Deviance Initiative. (2016). *Positive deviance definitions.* Accessed at www
.positivedeviance.org/about_pd/definitions-pd.html on August 23, 2016.

Reichelt, L. (2007, March 1). *Ambient intimacy* [Blog post]. Accessed at www
.disambiguity.com/ambient-intimacy on May 5, 2016.

Rick, T. (2014, June 11). *Organisational culture eats strategy for breakfast, lunch and dinner.* Accessed at www.torbenrick.eu/blog/culture/organisational-culture-eats -strategy-for-breakfast-lunch-and-dinner on January 25, 2016.

Rigor. (n.d.). In *Merriam-Webster Online Dictionary.* Accessed at www.merriam -webster.com/dictionary/rigor on May 5, 2016.

Ripley, A. (2008, November 26). Rhee tackles classroom challenge. *TIME.* Accessed at http://content.time.com/time/magazine/article/0,9171,1862444-1,00.html on May 5, 2016.

Rock, D. (2008). *SCARF: A brain-based model for collaborating with and influencing others.* Accessed at www.med.illinois.edu/depts_programs/academic_affairs /downloads/SCARF-NeuroleadershipArticle.pdf on July 16, 2016.

Rose, J. (2012). How to break free of our 19th-century factory-model education system. *The Atlantic.* Accessed at www.theatlantic.com/business/archive/2012/05 /how-to-break-free-of-our-19th-century-factory-model-education-system/256881 on July 25, 2016.

Rubin, B. C. (2012). *Making citizens: Transforming civic learning for diverse social studies classrooms.* New York: Routledge.

Schaps, E. (2005). *The role of supportive school environments in promoting academic success.* Accessed at www.collaborativeclassroom.org/research-articles-and-papers -the-role-of-supportive-school-environments-in-promoting-academic-success on July 26, 2016.

Schwartz, B. (2015). *Why we work.* New York: TEDBooks.

Seppala, E. (2016, February 2). A Stanford psychologist explains why spacing out and goofing off is so good for you. *The Washington Post.* Accessed at www.washingtonpost .com/news/inspired-life/wp/2016/02/02/a-stanford-psychologist-explains-why -spacing-out-and-goofing-off-is-so-good-for-you on February 2, 2016.

Shareski, D. (n.d.). *Joy (responses): Form responses 1.* Accessed at https://docs.google .com/spreadsheets/d/1jq53s8bYQeF4kpcoskgT8fdaVkA5D9HMxKWJRSks_wY /pubhtml on July 25, 2016.

Shareski, D. (2008). Student cellphone presentation. *Ideas and Thoughts.* Accessed at http://ideasandthoughts.org/2008/06/19/student-cellphone-presentation on July 26, 2016.

Shareski, D. (2011a, June 22). *Suck it up buttercup* [Video file]. Accessed at www .youtube.com/watch?v=pX3q7QDViu0 on December 30, 2015.

Shareski, D. [Dean Shareski]. (2011b, November 4). *What matters now.* Keynote presented at Tech Forum Texas in Austin, Texas. Accessed at www.slideshare.net /shareski/what-matters-now-10019451 on July 12, 2016.

Shareski, D. [shareski]. (2015a, December 31). *Do you do joy for joy's sake? Would love to have you respond. Please RT and share wildly!* [Tweet]. Accessed at https://twitter.com/shareski/statuses/682607678812631040?tw_ i=682607678812631040&tw_e=details&tw_p=archive&source=archive on July 25, 2016.

Shareski, D. [shareski]. (2015b, December 28). *How do you foster community in your classroom/school/district? Would love school examples #cpchat please RT* [Tweet]. Accessed at https://twitter.com/shareski/statuses/681532427794288640?tw_ i=681532427794288640&tw_e=details&tw_p=archive&source=archive on July 25, 2016.

Shareski, D. [Dean Shareski]. (2016, July 17). *Rob Fisher with Dylan* [Video file]. Accessed at www.youtube.com/watch?v=ngL5pMX1t8Q&feature=youtu .be on July 25, 2016.

Shirky, C. (2008). *Here comes everybody: The power of organizing without organizations.* New York: Penguin Press.

Shots of Awe. (2013, May 22). *Awe* [Video file]. Accessed at www.youtube.com /watch?v=8QyVZrV3d3o on January 29, 2016.

Siemens, G., Calder, J., Forgrave, A., Constantini, L., Kuropatwa, D., Wright, S., et al. (2011). *UnPlug'd: What matters most in education.* Toronto, Canada: UnPlug'd Canadian Education Summit.

Sivers, D. (n.d.). *Here comes everybody: By Clay Shirky.* Accessed at https://sivers.org /book/HereComesEverybody on January 31, 2016.

Smith, F. (1998). *The book of learning and forgetting.* New York: Teachers College Press.

Sparks, D., & Malkus, N. (2015). *Public school teacher autonomy in the classroom across school years 2003–04, 2007–08, 2011–12.* Accessed at http://nces.ed.gov /pubs2015/2015089.pdf on July 25, 2016.

Strauss, V. (2014, April 26). Kindergarten show canceled so kids can keep studying to become "college and career ready." Really. *The Washington Post.* Accessed at www .washingtonpost.com/news/answer-sheet/wp/2014/04/26/kindergarten-show -canceled-so-kids-can-keep-working-to-become-college-and-career-ready-really on January 27, 2016.

Suggate, S. P., Schaughency, E. A., & Reese, E. (2013). Children learning to read later catch up to children reading earlier. *Early Childhood Research Quarterly, 28*(1), 33–48.

TEDx Talks. (2013, July 1). *Whatever happened to joy in education?: Dean Shareski at TEDxWestVancouverED* [Video file]. Accessed at www.youtube.com/watch?v=qd -Nk2sB-vA on December 30, 2015.

Thomas, D., & Brown, J. S. (2011). *A new culture of learning: Cultivating the imagination for a world of constant change.* Lexington, KY: CreateSpace.

Tippett, K. (Producer). (2014, June 19). *On being: Play, spirit, and character* [Audio podcast]. Accessed at www.onbeing.org/program/play-spirit-and-character/143 on July 26, 2016.

Vaughn, N. [Nate Vaughn]. (2009, November 20). *I'm just waiting for some Miley* [Video file]. Accessed at www.youtube.com/watch?v=hEUh14_jLbQ on January 25, 2016.

Walker, T. (2015, October 1). The joyful, illiterate kindergartners of Finland: Forget the Common Core, Finland's youngsters are in charge of determining what happens in the classroom. *The Atlantic.* Accessed at www.theatlantic.com /education/archive/2015/10/the-joyful-illiterate-kindergartners-of-finland /408325 on January 27, 2016.

White, R. E. (2012). *The power of play: A research summary on play and learning.* Accessed at www.childrensmuseums.org/images/MCMResearchSummary.pdf on July 16, 2016.

Wiggins, G. (2014, October 10). *A veteran teacher turned coach shadows 2 students for 2 days—a sobering lesson learned* [Blog post]. Accessed at https://grantwiggins .wordpress.com/2014/10/10/a-veteran-teacher-turned-coach-shadows-2-students -for-2-days-a-sobering-lesson-learned on May 5, 2016.

Williams, D. (2013, November 4). *The story of how I found my joy* [Blog post]. Accessed at http://teacherdiana.com/?p=731 on August 29, 2016.

Willis, J. (2014, July 18). *The neuroscience behind stress and learning* [Blog post]. Accessed at www.edutopia.org/blog/neuroscience-behind-stress-and-learning -judy-willis on January 27, 2016.

WNYC. (2012, July 30). *Billy Joel* [Audio podcast]. Accessed at www.wnyc.org/story /225651-billy-joel on January 25, 2016.

Woof, B. (n.d.). *About FalconPLog.* Accessed at https://falconplog.wordpress.com /about-falconplog on January 29, 2016.

Solutions for Creating the Learning Spaces Students Deserve

Solutions Series: Solutions for Creating the Learning Spaces Students Deserve reimagines the norms defining K–12 education. In a short, reader-friendly format, these books challenge traditional thinking about schooling and encourage readers to question their beliefs about what real teaching and learning look like in action.

Creating a Culture of Feedback
by William M. Ferriter and Paul J. Cancellieri
BKF731

Embracing a Culture of Joy
by Dean Shareski
BKF730

Making Learning FLow
by John Spencer
BKF733

Reimagining Literacy Through Global Collaboration
by Pernille Ripp
BKF732

Wait! Your professional development journey doesn't have to end with the last pages of this book.

We realize improving student learning doesn't happen overnight. And your school or district shouldn't be left to puzzle out all the details of this process alone.

No matter where you are on the journey, we're committed to helping you get to the next stage.

Take advantage of everything from **custom workshops** to **keynote presentations** and **interactive web and video conferencing**. We can even help you develop an action plan tailored to fit your specific needs.

Let's get the conversation started.

Call 888.763.9045 today.

SolutionTree.com